Praise for
UPSTREAM: A Voyage on the Connecticut River

"Ben Bachman in UPSTREAM: A Voyage on the Connecticut River takes us on a journey from the mouth at Old Saybrook to the source in the wilderness of New Hampshire along the Canadian border . . . . Interspersed throughout the narrative are vignettes of river history and of events that have taken place along the shores."
—Edmund Delaney, The Connecticut Watershed Council

" . . . A combination of geology, natural history, and social history, an engaging, congenial narrative that meanders much like the river itself . . . full of descriptive paragraphs that sing. He has a wonderful knack of making you feel that you are riding in the canoe with him."
—The *West Hartford News*

" . . . A graceful, unassuming, vastly knowledgeable account that has everything going for it. Bachman is always worth listening to, and he never flaunts his expertise . . . a sharp-eyed, wide-ranging testimony to a rich regional piety."
—*Kirkus Reviews*

"Bachman, who has written for *Country Journal* and other magazines, is a pleasant and knowledgeable guide with a finely tuned sense of the region's history and ecology . . . . Of great regional interest, *Upstream* will appeal to readers who enjoy the outdoors."
—*Publishers Weekly*

"*Upstream* is also diverse, mixing a skillful blend of history, hydrology, canoe lore, and sharp observation of the passing scene."
—*American Land Forum*

"Bachman views the river and its valley with affection, with understanding, and always with fascination. Recommended particularly for public libraries in the New England Region."
—*Library Journal*

UPSTREAM

A Voyage on the Connecticut River

BEN BACHMAN

The Globe Pequot Press   Chester, Connecticut

Published Fall 1988 by The Globe Pequot Press
© 1985 by Ben Bachman.
Reprinted by special arrangement with Houghton Mifflin
Company.

Library of Congress
Library of Congress Cataloging–in–Publication Data

Bachman, Ben.
    Upstream : a voyage on the Connecticut River / Ben
Bachman. — 1st Globe Pequot ed.
        p. cm.
    Reprint. Originally published: Boston : Houghton
Mifflin, 1985.
    ISBN 0-87106-678-5
    1. Connecticut River—Description and travel.
2. Connecticut River Valley—Description and travel.
3. Bachman, Ben—Journeys—Connecticut River. I. Title.
[F12.C7B18   1988]
917.4′0443—dc 19   88-16332
                                                             CIP

Manufactured in the United States of America
First Edition / Second Printing

✒ Contents

ᗰ *Introduction*

*I*T WAS ALASKA that first got me interested in the Connecticut River. I have lived in the Connecticut Valley most of my life, but it was on a month-long trip down the Noatak River in Alaska that my passion for rivers was first awakened. Until then, a river was something to be crossed on a bridge. I had spent, perhaps, a grand total of no more than two hours in canoes, exclusively on ponds. I wasn't even sure how to hold a paddle, much less how to run a rapid. The Noatak was a grand adventure, and when I got back I bought a canoe of my own, then looked for a place to use it. The Connecticut River was the closest body of water, and after I had been out on it a few times I began to see it with new eyes.

When I was growing up in Hartford, the Connecticut had a rather unsavory reputation. It seemed to be a weary old river, a river that had been used hard and used badly, an industrial river. Fortunately the Connecticut has been cleaned up since that time, and although clean water was a pleasant discovery, there was more. Despite the fact that the Connecticut Valley has been settled by white men since the mid-seventeenth century and that New England has long been one of the most densely populated regions in the United States, the Connecticut River still threads a largely pastoral countryside, where frequent echoes of wildness, if not the vanished wilderness, linger on. Indeed, if one wanted to study the urbanization of New England (an absorbing subject in its own right), the view from a canoe on the Connecticut would not provide much enlightenment, since the river, for the most part, flows through a green and leafy corridor of solitude. This was a very pleasant discovery too, but it was just an added attraction. It was the river itself — its flow, its soul, its moods, and its raw power — that ultimately captured my full attention.

The Connecticut River rises from a tiny pond a few hundred yards from the Canadian border, in the northernmost tip of New Hampshire, and flows southward for some 400 miles to empty into Long Island Sound. The drainage basin covers about 11,500 square miles, encompassing parts of Connecticut, Massachusetts, Vermont, New Hampshire, and Québec. If a certain tributary near the headwaters was just a quarter-mile longer than it is, Maine would be included in the watershed as well. The Connecticut is a large river compared to most streams in the Northeast, but puny compared to the Columbia or the St. Lawrence or even to some minor tributaries of the Mississippi. And the mighty Mississippi, the Father of Waters, is a modest stream compared to the greatest river on earth, the Amazon. The Amazon's flow, at its mouth, is a staggering 620 million cubic feet per second, twice that of the Congo River and ten times as great as the Mississippi's flow. The Amazon is awesome. It is in a class by itself. Yet there is some of the Amazon's stupendous power in all rivers, including the Connecticut, because every stream on the planet is part of the same global system; all of them draw their waters from the same source, the oceans, and that water is in continual circulation: from sea to atmosphere, to mountains and plains, and back to the sea again. A river is unlike most other landscape forms; it is less a thing than a process. Its essence is movement. A river may be old, like the Connecticut, but in another sense it is eternally young, because the flow is always being renewed, endlessly, from one second to the next. As the Greek philosopher Heraclitus said, no man can step in the same river twice.

On the other hand, all rivers use the same water. The water in the Connecticut today has previously flowed down the Amazon (and the Nile and the Rhine and the Mekong) at some time in the past, and it will flow down those streams again in the future. So Heraclitus might just as well have said that when you have seen one river you have seen them all. Yet every river is unique, just as the landscape through which it flows is unique. Running water, in fact, is one of the great shapers of landscape. Over millions of years, a river leaves an intricate and distinctive mark upon the land, throughout the length and breadth of the watershed, and that mark, although constantly changing as erosion slowly wears away at the hills and deepens the valleys, is enduring enough to seem permanent to men. So the river, although reborn every instant, also has a legacy etched in stone.

Suffice it to say that a river is mysterious. It is always different and it is ever the same. It can never be fully understood. It is possible, however, to build a relationship with a river, but it takes time. I knew from my experience in Alaska that a month is not nearly long enough. I knew also that an end-to-end canoe trip is not necessarily the best approach. When you are paddling day in and day out it is the trip itself, not the river, that is most important. The desire to make miles, to keep moving, becomes overwhelming. So on the Connecticut I confined my explorations to manageable segments, caring more about the time I spent than the distance I covered, feeling free to go back for a second or third look, visiting the river in all seasons. I traveled mostly by canoe but used other means where it seemed appropriate, and I began where the river begins — not at its official source on the Canadian border, but out to sea, where this and every other river first draws the breath of life.

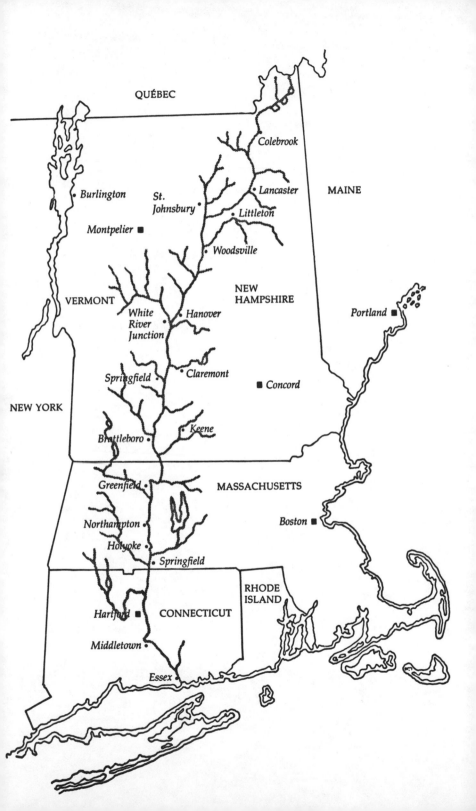

Upstream

1 ❧ SAYBROOK
to HARTFORD

The Long Tidal River

*T*HE TUGBOAT *Texaco Houma II* — eight hours out of Bayonne, New Jersey, and bound for Hartford, Connecticut — is plowing east across Long Island Sound, pushing a 300-foot oil barge. The midnight passage through New York Harbor and up the East River to the Hell Gate, timed to match the tide, is well behind us; it is now seven-thirty in the morning. The mouth of the Connecticut River is still six and a half hours ahead. Arrival in Hartford should be about eight or nine P.M., depending on how much ice we encounter in the river.

Houma is a noisy boat, and the vibration of the two General Motors/Electro-Motive Division diesels is felt clearly up here in the wheelhouse, four decks above the engine room, three above the waterline. Aside from that, however, all is calm; the marine radio is silent, and the radar screen shows no other ships within a radius of 12 miles. There is just the faintest suggestion of a swell, a gentle rise and fall of the sea like the heartbeat of a hibernating animal, and the overcast January sky is soft and gray. A lone gull rides on the mast of the barge, feathers puffed up against the cold. The Connecticut shoreline, when visible at all, is an indistinct smudge on the horizon.

Richy, the deckhand on watch, sits on the captain's high, padded stool with his slippered feet propped up on the chart table. The rest of the crew, except for the cook, are in their cabins. Richy is in charge, for the time being at least, a role he obviously enjoys. He is a short, muscular young man with weight-lifter arms and a thin gold chain around his neck. Although still in his twenties, he is starting to go bald on top.

With just me to talk to, Richy is subdued and reflective as our conversation turns to distant ports. The women of Murmansk impressed him; the sun-baked bleakness of Persian Gulf oil terminals did not. Richy has been at sea since he left high school in Bayonne, breaking in as a messboy on tankers and containerships; it is not easy to picture him in a little white jacket, waiting on officers. "Look," he says, "you have to start at the bottom. It was either that or McDonald's."

The tugboat job with Texaco Marine was definitely a step up. Virtually all tugboatmen claim to prefer coastal voyages to the grinding monotony of ocean crossings. *Houma* (registered in Wilmington, Delaware, but based in Bayonne) goes to such places as Albany, Hartford, Providence, Boston, and Portland, Maine. The crew lives on board for a week, then gets a week off — working, in effect, six months of the year. So the hours are right, if you don't mind pulling the three A.M. watches, and once the tug clears the harbor there is ample opportunity to get a lot of reading done, although one person, at the very least, has to maintain a high degree of alertness. The barge that *Houma* is pushing is full of no-lead gasoline; an accident could be catastrophic.

Out on the Sound rain has begun to fall again, adding to the puddles that have already collected on the flat metal deck of the barge. All New England has been socked in for the past three days. Brooks up in the hills, swollen with runoff refused by the frozen ground, have burst free from their customary winter cover of ice, and as the rivulets empty into the subtributaries and the subtributaries into the tributaries, which in turn empty into the master stream, the Connecticut River itself will rise, and the water will pass down to the sea, only to be lifted into the atmosphere once more. The hydrologic cycle is ceaseless. Yet of all the vast quantity of water that evaporates from the surface of the oceans, almost all of it falls back into the oceans again as rain, without ever nurturing an inland river. The smallest blip in this pattern produces noticeable fluctuations in stream flow. Indeed, flooding is predicted in Connecticut.

The flood, if it actually occurs, will subside soon enough. Far out in the middle of the Atlantic Ocean another process is taking place, so slowly as to be invisible but with important consequences for rivers nevertheless. Beginning near the North Pole, a long ridge like a great range of submarine mountains runs south to Iceland, where it surfaces briefly, then continues for thousands of miles, almost to Antarctica. Along the entire ridge magma is continually rising from the earth's mantle and spreading to form new sea floor. As it does, the sea floor already in place on either side of the midocean ridge is pushed outward, to the west and to the east, and this in turn causes North America to move to the west while Eurasia moves to the east. The Atlantic Ocean, in other words, is getting wider, and this sea floor spreading is one of the basic mechanisms of plate tectonics. As the plates move they grind together, or slide along one another, and portions of sea floor are subducted under the continental land masses, passing back down into the mantle. The Pacific Ocean, for example, is getting smaller in reaction to the widening of the Atlantic. In addition, the tremendous forces generated by the movements and the collisions of the plates cause mountains to be raised; this is the critical part as far as rivers are concerned. Without periodic episodes of mountain building, running water would wear down all the existing mountains to a level plain, and there would be few, if any, rivers left on earth.

But mountains do not disappear overnight. The last major era of mountain building in New England took place about 350 million years ago, when all the land masses on the planet came together to form the supercontinent of Panagea. About 140 million years ago Panagea began to split, and the infant Atlantic Ocean first appeared. The history of the Connecticut River can be traced back to the breakup of Panagea as well, for it was then that the ancestral drainage patterns of the present river began to take shape. The Atlantic has been widening ever since, slowly but steadily, a few centimeters each year, the process continuing even as *Texaco Houma* leaves a rolling wake in Long Island Sound.

The rain has shown no sign of letting up, either, and at nine o'clock Kevin, the mate, relieves Richy at the helm. About an hour later the captain, Jeff Maynard, climbs the wheelhouse stairs with a cup of coffee in his hand to look things over. There are no problems. With a blank horizon and calm seas, *Houma* is well out of harm's way, but Jeff, a self-contained man who never raises his voice, stays for a while to talk and to watch. Then the chief engineer pays a rare visit from belowdeck, and the atmosphere in the wheelhouse begins to resemble that of a reunion. Even on a boat as small as *Houma*, crew members on different watches can go for a day at a time, or longer, without speaking to one another. The two-man barge crew is in another world entirely, communicating with the tug by radio.

At noon we eat a chicken dinner, sitting down to the small galley table in shifts, and shortly before two P.M. the lighthouse at the mouth of the Connecticut River appears off the port bow. As we come closer, it is clear that there are two lighthouses: a tall one (with a steady white light) on the mainland and a short stubby one (with a flashing green light) at the end of a long breakwater. As the tug swings the barge around to a northerly heading to enter the channel, the white light appears to move until it is directly above the flashing green. "That's how you know you're lined up right," Kevin says. The tide is ebbing at present, allowing the Connecticut's current to push a fan of silt far out into the Sound. This is a powerful river. The average monthly rate of discharge is 333 cubic meters per second, greater than that of the Hudson, the Delaware, or the Potomac, and about half that of the Susquehanna.

The big summer places on the point are closed for the season, although a girl with an Irish setter is jogging along the desolate beach. Glum clouds press down on the low hills in the distance, and water beads on the wheelhouse windows, the droplets inching across the glass in sync with *Houma*'s drumming engines. As we slide by the breakwater, slowing to meet the pilot boat, the Old Lyme salt marshes pass by to starboard. The marsh is alive during the warmer months with clapper rails, fiddler crabs, muskrats, ospreys, and great flocks of delicate, skittering shorebirds — the "wind birds," Peter Matthiessen calls them — that lift off the tide flats like puffs of noisy smoke, swooping and banking in perfect unison before landing at your feet, if you stand still enough, and going to sleep, laying their heads back on a wing.

But the peeps have long since fled to South America. The crabs are buried in the mud, and ice skims the marsh creeks. The lush stands of *Spartina patens* are dead, brown and matted in the wan light. Duck blinds stick up like pillboxes on an abandoned battlefield. In *Houma*'s wheelhouse, all attention has shifted to the little pilot boat, which looks even smaller now that it is beside the ponderous bulk of the barge. Richy, who has pulled on oilskins, is out on the deck holding the ladder for Alan, the pilot, a skinny, black-haired man dressed in Calvin Klein jeans, Top-Siders, and a Navy pea coat. The pilot boat

5

veers away, and a few minutes later *Houma* is bearing down on the Amtrak drawbridge that crosses the Connecticut from Saybrook to Lyme. The bridgetender tells us to come ahead, then quickly changes his mind.

"Hold it up a second, Cap," he says over the radio. "I've got an eastbound train on the way." The bridgetender works for the railroad; trains get preference. Steamboat companies managed to prevent the construction of a bridge here — and elsewhere on the lower Connecticut — until the mid-1870s. Eventually the railroad (the powerful New York, New Haven & Hartford) bought all the steamboats. The train we are waiting for comes along shortly, clattering over the river, and then the massive, double-track Bascule drawspan begins to open. *Houma*'s chrome-plated, compressed-air-activated throttle controls hiss as Alan shoves them both to the full-ahead position, and the bow pushes hard against the big V-shaped notch in the stern of the barge, gathering momentum, the tachometer needles quivering as the rpm's climb and the propellers (the "wheels," in tugboat jargon) bite into the water, working against current and tide.

Two boys are standing on a dock in the rain, taking our picture. Out on the Sound the tug was in its own element, a completely unremarkable sight, but here on the river, in a world of dripping woods and ordinary back yards, we are something of an exotic visitor. Before *Houma* gets back to Bayonne we will be stared at, waved at, and videotaped by a television news crew out with the Coast Guard on an icebreaker. There is something about the sight of this tug pushing a barge up the river that makes everyone stop and look. During the eighteenth century, however, there was a good deal more traffic on the river, and many of the vessels were built nearby. Along the lower Connecticut, some forty yards turned out a grand total of four thousand merchant ships as well as small craft, yachts, privateers, and men-of-war, including the 700-ton, 36-gun frigate

Trumbull. The *Trumbull* was launched in 1776 but no ship of her size was ever built at a river yard again, and by the time the age of clipper ships began, almost all shipbuilding activity in the valley had ceased. Connecticut River captains continued to sail the world, however, and they built handsome Georgian and Greek Revival mansions for their wives and families in river towns like Essex, Lyme, and the Haddams.

A ferocious sort of fastidiousness holds sway in the Essex of the 1980s; even the gas stations fit the prevailing architecture. The narrow main street is clogged with expensive German automobiles, and the waterfront is a forest of aluminum masts in July. In January, as *Texaco Houma* steams by, there appears to be plenty of moorage space available. We are starting to see birds now, and the wheelhouse binoculars are passed back and forth to examine large dark objects in distant trees, which turn out to be squirrel nests. A few bald eagles winter along the lower Connecticut, but they seem to be somewhere else today. Cormorants are sitting on rocks and buoys, spreading their black wings to dry, and a great blue heron is walking around stiffly on a large pan of drifting ice. According to the distribution maps in Frank G. Belrose's authoritative *Ducks, Geese and Swans of North America*, it should be possible to observe at least fifteen species of wintering waterfowl here. We are encountering mainly common mergansers by the thousands, in small groups and vast flocks, perhaps with some red-breasted mergansers also. Mergansers take flight at the slightest provocation — the tug is definitely a major provocation — but as *Houma* bores steadily upstream, three imperious mute swans glide out from the shore on a collision course with the barge, refusing to grant right of way until the last possible instant.

Alan gets a kick out of this, as he does out of most things. He crackles with excess energy, like a high-strung bird dog scrabbling around in the back of a station wagon. He steers standing up, bouncing up and down a little on the balls of his feet in front of an open wheelhouse window, the wind and rain blowing in on his face. He is too busy talking and gesticulating to pay any attention to the transistor radio he brought on board in his overnight bag. *Texaco Houma* does not have a steering wheel; the rudder is controlled by an innocuous-looking lever about 5 inches long that slides across the wheelhouse on a metal track according to where the pilot wants to stand — an important feature during docking operations. Alan keeps one hand on this device, casually. From the unconcerned look on his face, he could just as well be driving a car down an empty freeway. He is not, of course. Piloting calls for skill, good judgment, and calm nerves. Alan's fidgety manner is deceptive; watch him for a while and you see that the man knows exactly what he is doing. All his maneuvers are thought out well in advance, as they have to be. The barge takes up a tremendous amount of space, almost as much as a football field, and it cannot be turned or stopped in anything like a hurry.

Running aground is not a major worry as long as a pilot keeps to the channel. Our barge draws 10 feet 3 inches in salt water, 10 feet 6 inches in fresh, and the Army Corps of Engineers "project depth" for the navigation channel is 15 feet. This does not mean that the river is only 15 feet deep — in many places it is much deeper — but the riverbed has an undulating profile, something like a series of riffles and pools in a trout stream, and the main current is continually piling up bars as it weaves back and forth from one side of the river to the other in response to curves in the course. (Actually, the current is in large part responsible for creating the curves, but that's another story.) Dredging the navigation channel is a year-round necessity. Buoys mark fixed obstructions, and numbered beacons — more than a hundred between Saybrook and Hartford — appear along the banks every few miles. Even so, a pilot's best navigation aid is his own knowledge of the river. He has to know what it's like at high water and low. He has to know every peculiarity of tide and current. He has to know what the bottom is like, and he has to know where to expect sudden gusts of wind. An empty barge is particularly susceptible to crosswinds.

In the summer and fall, the river generates early morning fogs so intense that visibility closes down to a few feet. Even with radar, the only safe course is to stop. If the bottom will hold, you can anchor, or perhaps the barge can be moored to a sturdy tree. Another solution is to "plant" the bow of the barge on the muddy shore of an island, but that can be risky. Alan likes to tell about one pilot who aimed his barge, let it go, and then watched it run up on the beach . . . and continue into the woods, knocking over trees like matchsticks. "He was lucky," Alan said. "People camp on those islands. He could have killed someone."

"Look," Alan says now, pointing to an elderly woman in an ankle-length fur coat who is watching us from the end of a short dock. "That lady always comes out to wave. She'll be there in a blizzard." A little farther upstream I scan a hillside with binoculars and meet the gaze of a man and a woman standing in their living room, snug behind floor-to-ceiling plate glass. A fire is crackling on a fieldstone hearth. But there aren't many houses along this stretch of river. Flat land where a house could be built is scarce. The hills rise directly out of the water and climb up 200 or 300 feet, sometimes in slabby, broken cliffs. It is a bold landscape and a relatively young one, too, in geological terms. The lower Connecticut used to follow a more westerly course, emptying into the ocean in the vicinity of New Haven (where the outlines of the ancient, gentle valley can still be traced). It will be several million years before the river creates a broad floodplain along its "new" course, and now, as the light begins to drain out of the somber January sky, the valley could almost pass for primeval wilderness. It could almost be the same valley that the Dutch explorer Adrian Block saw when he navigated these waters in 1614.

Block was not a total stranger to the region, having already made one voyage to North America. During the second trip he spent the winter of 1613–1614 on Manhattan Island, where his ship burned to the waterline. The replacement vessel, a ketch-rigged "yacht" 44½ feet long, was built from timbers felled along Wall Street; this was the boat Block sailed up Long Island Sound and then up the Connecticut. At that time the Indians called the river Quinnehtukgut, "the Long Tidal River" or simply "the Long River." Block named it De Vershe Riviere, "the Freshwater River." Evidently he was not one to be carried away by wild flights of poetic fancy. His main interest in the New World was economic — he had been hired by a group of Amsterdam merchants to set up a fur trade with the Indians — but surely he must have indulged in some gawking as well, for this was a place to amaze European eyes. Back home in Holland, and in England, too, most of the timber had long since been cut, the land cultivated, and every wild animal larger than a fox or a badger exterminated. Here there were moose, bears, and wolves, beavers in every stream, rivers full of 10-pound salmon, and white pines 200 feet tall. The entire Connecticut watershed, not to mention the rest of the continent, was a pristine wilderness of shining lakes and dark forest. Block sampled only a small part of it. After visiting some Indian villages, he continued upstream to Enfield, some 60 miles inland, where rapids forced him to turn back. He never laid eyes on his De Vershe Riviere again. A few of his countrymen later established trading posts on the lower river, but they were evicted by English settlers from Massachusetts. There was to be no lasting Dutch presence on the Connecticut, as there was on the Hudson. Yet Block was the first white man to come here. That cannot be taken away from him.

∾

"Stanley Mitchel is the man you should talk to," Alan says. "He's the last of the old steamboat pilots. You should hear his stories. Those old pilots used to run in the fog with a stopwatch and a compass — so many seconds on one heading, then switch to the next. They had it all figured out. They knew the river blindfolded."

No doubt they did, but that did not preclude accidents. In 1876, for example, the steamboat *City of Hartford* struck the new railroad drawbridge in Middletown while running at night. The impact of the collision carried away several of the fixed truss spans, draping one of them over the vessel's foredeck. Altogether, some thirty-five large steamboats were in service on the Connecticut River, mainly on the Hartford–New York City route, between 1822 and 1931. At one point Hartford could boast two thousand steamboat arrivals and departures in a year. As a result of price wars, the fare to New York hit a low of 50 cents one way, including meals (although that did not last very long). It is probably fair to say that the 279-foot, 814-ton *City of Hartford* was the quintessential Connecticut River steamboat. Unlike the tubby, wedding-cake dowagers on the Mississippi, she was an aristocratic sidewheeler with a knife-blade bow, clean lines, and chaste white paint. The *Hartford Courant* described the passenger accommodations:

> Her cabins and saloons are very spacious and elegantly fitted up with carpets of Brussells and velvet tapestry, in glorious patterns, curtains of satin brocatelle, rosewood chairs, sofas and settees, very easy and of beautiful and appropriate patterns, covered with the same material, rosewood tables and sideboards with marble tops, etc., etc., etc. On the upper deck are some thirty-five staterooms of different sizes, some opening into others for the accommodation of families, all splendidly curtained and furnished — and two large "Bridal Rooms," in appearance rich enough to satisfy a prince.

Rebuilt as the *Capitol City* after the Middletown disaster, she finally struck a ledge and sank in a gale off Rye, New York, in 1886. Still larger boats took her place on the river, including the

1,488-ton, propeller-driven *Hartford* and the 1,554-ton *Middletown*, but railroads were cutting into steamboat passenger traffic, and the Depression finished it off. The *Hartford* made her last trip to New York on October 31, 1931. Gasoline and fuel oil still come up the Connecticut in barges, pushed by diesel tugs like *Houma*, and small coastal tankers that Alan calls "power boats" also navigate the river. At present, Texaco is the only oil company using its own vessels on the Hartford run; the rest of the traffic is handled by independent tugboat companies.

To the best of Alan's knowledge, there are no other tugs moving on the river tonight. Nevertheless, he announces *Houma*'s position on the radio each time we swing around a blind curve, just to be on the safe side. The East Haddam bridgetender knows we are coming, too; he has the drawspan open and *Houma* passes through without slowing down. A mile or two upstream the 600-megawatt Haddam nuclear plant appears on the right bank, illuminated by floodlights and exhaling a few wisps of steam. Built in the 1960s, when chambers of commerce still burbled about "atoms for peace," it lacks the heavy, sinister mass of a Three Mile Island or a Diablo Canyon. At the time, environmentalists were primarily concerned with what the plant's cooling system might do to the river, specifically to the fish, since this part of the Connecticut, which is tidal (but much less salty than the Sound), is extremely rich in estuarine life. An impact study identified more than fifty different species of fish in the immediate vicinity, including menhaden, white perch, alewives, killifish, shad, pike, suckers, large-mouth bass, striped bass, bluefish, and the like. As expected, large numbers of fish were attracted to the flow of warm water from the cooling system at the mouth of the outlet canal, and apparently they were quite happy to be there, many of them lingering in the canal throughout the winter. A more pressing worry was how the warm water might affect fish passing by the plant on annual migrations or spawning runs.

The great Connecticut River salmon runs ended long ago, in the late eighteenth century, when rapidly proliferating dams on upstream tributaries closed off access to the spawning grounds in quick-running, gravel-bottomed mountain brooks. However, in the 1960s a substantial number of shad — the so-called poor man's salmon — still made their way up the Connecticut each spring. The American shad is actually a member of the herring, not the salmonoid, family. Roe shad (the females) weigh as much as 5 or 6 pounds, bucks a bit less. The shad is a very bony fish, which caused it to be shunned in colonial times, but now both the flesh and the eggs are considered a great delicacy, and the May spawning runs have become a major event, an occasion for fishing derbies and community shad suppers. There is a commercial shad fishery, too, which employs about a hundred seasonal fishermen. Big gill nets that drift with the current at night, when the shad can't see the mesh, are the preferred commercial gear.

Because water temperature is one of the factors that seems to control shad behavior during the spawning run, it was feared that the "thermal plume" — the warm water — from the power plant might confuse the shad, perhaps by creating an invisible barrier that would cause them to tarry in the area or even to turn back. It might also interfere with the young shad swimming downstream to the Sound. (A few adults return to the Sound, too; they are called "racers.") To date, however, none of these things appear to have happened, and in fact the size of the run has increased a little, thanks to pollution control and the construction of fish ladders on dams above Hartford.

As *Texaco Houma* puts the East Haddam nuke behind the stern, we begin to encounter extensive ice. There has been drift ice in the river all along, but up ahead there is no open water at all; the ice stretches from bank to bank. I watch Alan to see what he plans to do. Apparently nothing. When the bow of the barge smashes into the ice our speed is immediately cut in half, but

13

the engines never miss a beat. The ice, it seems, is fairly soft and breaks into chunks that rumble along the bottom of the hull, producing a new up-and-down motion in the deck under our feet. Big white pieces of ice bob to the surface in *Houma's* boiling wake.

The passage above Haddam, known as the Narrows, is spectacular by daylight, and even in the dark. It must have been even nicer before high-tension lines were strung across the river from metal towers on the cliff tops and before the big Northeast Utilities oil-fired plant was built on the west bank. Middletown, at the head of the Narrows, was once a busy port, larger than Hartford in the early years, and a manufacturing center as well, but the blush of prosperity has faded. The shipyards across the river in Portland (where the frigate *Trumbull* slid down the ways) are hardly a memory, and the rusty swing-span railroad drawbridge (a descendant of the bridge struck by the *City of Hartford* in 1876) stands open all day and all night. There is no bridgetender. As we pass close to one of the ancient stone piers, breaking ice, Alan tells me that on Halloween night a few years back some teenagers released the brakes on a string of boxcars, letting them coast out onto the open drawbridge and into the river. One car, with its doors sealed shut, floated a mile and a half downstream.

All the way from Saybrook to Middletown we had been following a northwesterly course; now the river has swung around a sharp curve and *Houma* is heading due north (if you disregard short-term kinks and eccentric meandering bends). Were it not for the foul weather and the darkness, it would be apparent that the valley has changed character also, becoming much, much broader. The fiord-like cliffs of the Narrows have given way to a gentle alluvial floodplain. This is the Connecticut's ancestral valley, a landscape that dates back at least 100 million years into the early post-Panagean era, when the young Atlantic Ocean was just a few hundred miles wide and dinosaurs roamed New England. In more recent times, nineteenth-century steamboat tourists were impressed by the fertile soil and the platoons of young women in long dresses working in the onion fields. Tobacco — premium leaf used for cigar wrappers — became a big crop between about 1910 and 1955, and hundreds of abandoned tobacco barns still dot the valley today as far north as Greenfield, Massachusetts.

Passing by Rocky Hill, Connecticut, 8 miles above Middletown, sleet and snow are beginning to mix with the pouring rain, but it is possible to spot the ferry, hauled out in a nearby boatyard for the winter. This ferry, and its predecessors, have run every summer since 1655. Tonight there is no open water between the two ferry slips — until *Houma* smashes out a channel with the barge. The ice is giving us no trouble, even as we go around the tight curves in the frequent meander loops. Alan has been on his feet for more than eight hours, constantly alert, and conversation starts to lag now as the empty coffee cups pile up. He still has one of the front windows open partway, but it is warm enough inside the darkened wheelhouse. A faint, pulsing orange glow emanates from the radar screen, and every fifteen minutes the brass clock above the chart table chimes softly. There is no moon. There are no stars. Periodically we pass a blinking red beacon, but mostly the view ahead is wet, inky black night. When he feels the need, Alan switches on one of *Houma*'s brilliant searchlights and plays it back and forth across the river, looking for logs or stumps lodged in the ice. The beam picks up driving snow, startled flights of birds, and, at one point near Glastonbury, a car creeping down a slick, narrow road along the bank. As we bear down on it the vehicle stops. Then it backs up. Suddenly I have a vision of what the driver must be seeing: *Houma*'s red and green running lights, the probing eye of the searchlight, and the immense black hull of the barge, rumbling and groaning as it shoves the ice aside.

Forty-five minutes later *Houma* arrives in Hartford — in East

Hartford, to be precise. The river separates the two cities, East Hartford being to Hartford as Camden is to Philadelphia or Hoboken is to New York: a necessary place, a city of machine shops, beer distributors, union halls, and tank farms, the kind of place where oil barges always tie up. Hartford has the opera and the NHL hockey team; East Hartford, the huge Pratt & Whitney jet engine factory. Jeff Maynard comes up from his cabin to supervise the docking. Richy and another deckhand pull on their insulated overalls, pull yellow slickers and pants on top of that, and go out into the storm, Jeff signaling to them with shrill blasts of the peep whistle as they wrestle the frozen mooring lines. The barge crew's work is just beginning; it will take all night to unload the gasoline.

When the lines are made fast to Jeff's satisfaction, the chief shuts down the diesels, and, except for the faint hum of a generator somewhere down in the engine room, *Houma* is quiet for the first time since we left Bayonne. Before turning in, I visit the galley for a corned beef sandwich and some deviled eggs and stay to watch the eleven o'clock news. The weather report still predicts local flooding, but the rain seems to be tapering off.

2 ❧ HARTFORD
to SPRINGFIELD

A Strong Brown God

*I*T WAS THE FIRST day of June, the nub of the morning rush hour, clear and sunny. Interstate 84 flowed like a river. The bow of my 17-foot Old Town canoe stuck out over the hood of the car; the bumper of a thundering dump truck filled the rearview mirror.

"Which exit are you going to take?" asked my father.

"This one," I said. "Right here." I was using the high-rise Ramada Inn as a landmark. We cut across three lanes of traffic, descended to street level, and detoured around a construction site. An unmarked dirt road led up over the top of a dike, and there was the Connecticut, wide and silty, swollen with runoff, the glass towers of Hartford rising from a brown swirl of freeways on the other side.

My father had dressed for a day at the office, and the boat ramp was coated with slick mud. I told him there was no need to dirty his shoes, so he stood there watching with an amused smile on his face, the expression of faint bewilderment that all men reserve for their sons, as I hoisted the canoe and carried it down to the water. I had invited him to join me on the river, but he dismissed the idea with a laugh, not having set foot in a canoe since his honeymoon in the Ozarks thirty-seven years before. He had agreed, however, to drive my car to Windsor Locks (about a dozen miles upstream) and pick me up at five o'clock in the afternoon. I stowed a bag lunch in the bow of the canoe and shoved off.

Hartford does not have a waterfront; it has not had one since the high dikes were built after the great flood of 1936. There are no rotting wharves, no old pilings, not much of anything, and it felt a little peculiar, almost as though I were trespassing, to be out here on the big river, looking up at the tall buildings, without another living soul in sight. The city gave off a dull, gritty roar. The river was about a third of a mile wide, but it narrowed ahead, where a rusty railroad bridge crossed the channel. The nine truss spans seemed to sit lightly, almost nervously, on their brownstone piers, and as I came closer the current began to surge. I could feel it in my shoulders, and I picked up the cadence, bending the paddle shaft a little on each stroke, carving out deep holes that floated off downstream as the brown water sluiced by the gunwales. But the canoe would not move forward; the best I could do was hold my own, like a runner on a treadmill. I swung the outboard motor into position and fired it up.

The turbulent wakes that streamed out below the bridge piers sent the canoe skidding sideways, the motor racing in the backwash and the eddies, then laboring as the prop bit into solid water, making headway slowly, foot by foot, suddenly spurting forward and slowing again, while I squatted in the bottom of the canoe, holding on to the center thwart to keep the bow down. The river grew wider upstream. A long, gradual bend curved around to the right, and when I looked back over my shoulder the Hartford skyline had vanished. There was no sign of the city at all. Thick woods came down to either bank.

The river is tidal at Hartford but not above it. From here on out, from Hartford to the headwaters, there is nothing — except dams — to interfere with the flow of the current, and there are few forces in nature so relentlessly single-minded as a river bent upon reaching the sea. This current, this great insistent shove of water gathered from a 12,000-square-mile watershed, is a factor to be reckoned with, a continual adversary that is unforgiving, pitiless, and indefatigable, a thing to be wondered at, its raw fluid power awesome and mysterious. The current *is* the river; it is the river's heart and soul, its pulse. In the spring, after the thaw, the pulse is strongest, almost exuberant, charged with snowmelt from the northern mountains. The freshet normally begins to taper off in June, as it was doing now, but more slowly this year than last, April and May having been exceptionally rainy. The river was still up in the trees at low places along the banks. Overhanging limbs snagged in the water and made sharp, hissing wakes. Logs, clumps of grass, and scraps of lumber swirled by the canoe, along with winged maple seeds and white fluff from the cottonwoods. The river was alive, a thing of motion and momentum, the depths murky and dense with a heavy load of silt, the surface blinding in the harsh glare of the sun, the racing water erupting in boils, indented with small whirlpools, veined and muscled with shifting ridges of current — a strong brown god, to use T. S. Eliot's phrase.

When Wallace Stevens worked in the claims department of a Hartford insurance Company he used to take lunchtime walks along the Connecticut's flood dikes, and I imagine that he watched the current streaming by. There is a hypnotic quality about the flow of a river; you can see whatever you care to in the moving water, but to appreciate the current fully you have to meet it head on, in a boat. Of course, I was cheating with the motor. I didn't know any better. At this stage in my river education, the idea of challenging the current without some sort of auxiliary power was too intimidating. I did not believe it was possible, and in fact there *are* pitches of current that can easily defeat paddlers far stronger than I, yet it is only after you try, and fail, again and again that you have sufficient motivation to study the flow and really begin to learn something about its behavior. The current is not simply a uniform mass of water in motion; at any given moment it is responding to dozens of different factors, and the river-wise canoeist will come to recognize these things, use them to his advantage, and work his way upstream with his wits as much as with his back and his arms.

For the time being, however, I was content to rely on the motor, and even that kept me occupied, avoiding logs. Also, the going was slow. A man walking along the bank could have left the canoe behind — had there been any place on the bank for a man to walk, which there was not. The woods were a tangled jungle of brush, deadfall, sumac, briars, ferns, and rank weeds. There were woody vines as thick as your wrist, and there was poison ivy. I have never seen the like of it. Dense, glossy mats of the stuff covered the ground and climbed up the trees to a height of 10 feet. Some of the cottonwoods were giants, with great thick trunks scarred by old ice jams and coated with the powdery brown silt of recent flooding. Spotted sandpipers walked lightly on the flotsam caught behind trees that had toppled into the water where the current had undercut the banks. Gulls from the Hartford dump sailed overhead and settled down on the river in rafts.

An hour went by, perhaps two hours. I wasn't keeping track. The air was still and hot, and the motor buzzed in my ear. It had a lulling effect and it smelled good — a nice, summery, nostalgic smell. If I closed my eyes, the canoe felt as if it was racing along; there was no sense of being held back.

A mile above the Bissel toll bridge, I came to the foot of a long narrow island close to the Connecticut's west bank. The river had spilled over into the woods, creating a temporary swamp. I shut off the motor and let the canoe glide between the trees, listening to the warblers, their bright, intense voices like noise squirted out of a tube. Clouds of mosquitoes soon drove me back into the open and I continued upstream, threading the narrow channel between the island and the mainland until arriving at the mouth of the Farmington River.

With a watershed of 600 square miles, the Farmington is the Connecticut's fourth largest tributary. It rises in the Berkshire Hills of western Massachusetts and provides good fly fishing and whitewater canoeing along much of its length, but the final few miles across flat bottomland are not terribly exciting. Still, it is hard to pass up any navigable waterway without making at least a cursory exploration, and in this case there was the additional lure of large concentrations of jumping fish. What was going on here? After a while the splashing tapered off — and then started again. There had to be an explanation. A mile up the Farmington, near the Loomis School, two men wearing business suits and rubber waders were casting from the bank. I asked one of them about the fish.

"Alewives," he said, then added that he was after shad and not having much luck. Like the shad, the alewife is an ocean-dwelling member of the herring family and a freshwater spawner. The alewife run reaches its peak in early June, overlapping the end of the shad run, although most anglers scorn alewives. They are small (about 10 to 12 inches long), bony, and oily. In colonial times the spawning alewives were taken from the rivers in nets by the ton, great silvery squirming masses of them hauled out and salted away for the winter or loaded in wagons to be shoveled on the fields as fertilizer,* but this practice has long since ended.

About 6 miles in from the Farmington's mouth, after placid wanderings across meadows and woods, the first set of rapids begins where the river threads a gap in a long line of bluffs. It

---

*Contrary to folklore, the Indians did not use fish as fertilizers.

is here on the tableland above these bluffs that shade tobacco —
an exotic, aromatic crop peculiar to the Connecticut Valley — is
making its last stand, down now to a couple of thousand acres
and sorely beleaguered by the decline of the domestic cigar industry, the impossible economics of land labor, and by the pressure of commercial real estate development, brought on by the
nature of the land itself (flat and vacant) and the proximity of
Bradley Field, the Hartford-Springfield airport. No other crop is
quite like shade tobacco; as a boy I remember what seemed to
be mile upon mile of filmy cheesecloth netting suspended above
the fields on hundreds of 9-foot cedar posts, with the roofs of
the barns sticking up like dark islands in a calm white sea. The
tobacco barns are long and narrow with louvered sides, the har-
vested leaves hung inside to dry in tiers, upside down, gradually turning brown. The netting, along with copious irrigation,
re-created the shady, humid conditions of Cuba and Sumatra.
Now air freight warehouses and insurance company data-proc-
essing centers have moved into the fields. Onetime country
roads throb with traffic, at nine and again at five, and private
cops in orange gloves and blaze orange vests, like deer hunters,
direct steady streams of Toyotas and Hondas in and out of the
parking lots. But it was peaceful enough in the canoe on the
Farmington River, aside from an occasional 747 sweeping low
over the valley on its final approach to the airport. At an altitude
of 700 feet, the big jets looked like remarkably authentic scale
models.

I paddled up to the foot of the rapids, then turned around
to drift back down to the mouth, where the alewives were still
jumping. There seemed to be more of them than before; the
steady noise of the splashing sounded like a gentle rain. Now
and then I spotted a flash of silver down in the murky depths
as an alewife rolled over on its side. Shading my eyes to cut the
surface glare, I looked for more fish and began to find them. It
was hard to believe at first, but the jumping alewives were just

the tip of the iceberg; for every fish that jumped there were hundreds, perhaps thousands, that did not. They were packed into dense, pulsing, endless schools from bank to bank, like a living conveyor belt. When I dipped my paddle into the water, alewives bumped against the blade.

Back out on the Connecticut a fresh wind had come up. High clouds were moving in, and the thick noontime heat had evaporated. Later in the summer, when the water drops, this part of the river gets quite shallow, exposing a maze of channels and sandbars, many of them awash or just inches beneath the surface, but there was no hint of that today. The river was a broad silver sheet, slightly ruffled by the wind, wide and majestic, looking as if it flowed on for another thousand miles. Even with the motor churning away at full power, it took fifteen minutes to cross to the east bank.

Holstein cows grazed in some partially cleared woods by the river's edge. Abandoned tobacco barns stood out in an open field, and beyond that a few house tops and a steeple poked through the trees in South Windsor, on a bluff about a mile away. Old John Bissel used to pasture his cattle in these meadows, and before long I came to the former site of the Bissel ferry landing, near the mouth of the Scantic River. Bissel's ferry, which began crossing the Connecticut between South Windsor and Windsor in 1641, was the first officially chartered ferry on the river and may well have been the first in the country. Bissel built a house here in 1658, and there was a small sawmill next door for a while, as well as a shipyard that built sailing vessels for the West Indian trade. The house became a tavern in 1816. The South Windsor jail and poor farm occupied the premises later but are gone now. The Bissel house is still standing, along with a cluster of barns and outbuildings, and while eighteenth- (and even seventeenth-) century houses are by no means scarce in this part of the state (Windsor, Hartford, and Wethersfield having been settled in the 1630s), few of the old homesteads have such a splendidly isolated location. This scene by the river cannot look too much different than it did two hundred and fifty years ago. In fact, this reach of the Connecticut is probably quieter now than it was in the 1700s.

The wind was witching around, gusting and dying off. Brush and trees sticking out of the water betrayed the presence of a number of small islands. This is a fine place for ducks and geese in the fall, but gulls were the only birds active now. Half an hour passed, and the massive I-91 bridge appeared in the distance.

I passed the boat ramp where I was supposed to meet my father. He wasn't there yet, so I continued up to the bridge and nosed the canoe into the bottom lock of the Windsor Locks canal. The 6-mile-long canal, no longer used for navigation but still in fairly good repair, was built to take boats around Enfield Rapids, which begin about a half-mile upstream. The second lock gate was open, and by standing in the canoe, I could just see over the top of the third gate — a heavy wooden affair with concrete counterweights — into the still water above. The locks were barely wide enough to turn the canoe around in without touching the brownstone walls. The water in the second lock was about a foot deep. My 14-foot setting pole would not touch bottom in the first lock.

☙

While I was inspecting the locks, an Amtrak passenger train went by on the tracks beside the canal, which gave me the idea of continuing my river journey by rail. I drove to Windsor Locks the next morning, the second of June, and pulled into the gravel parking lot by the new station, a small plastic hutch, on the outskirts of town. With the train to Springfield due at 11:22 I had a few minutes to wait, so I stepped across the tracks to take a look at the river.

The alewives were jumping. There didn't seem to be as many as the day before, but that there should be any at all, after

the thousands that had gone and were still going up the Farmington River, seemed remarkable. These alewives at Windsor
Locks, having already made their way 60 miles up the Connecticut from the Sound, now faced the most taxing part of the trip,
the 6-mile ascent of Enfield Rapids. I could appreciate the effort
involved because I had tried to climb the rapids in the canoe the
previous November. It was, as I recall, a cold morning with a
sooty sky and a stinging headwind that spat rain, not the best
conditions for a river outing, but, given my level of ignorance
about what I was attempting to do, the weather made little difference. I had read somewhere that the proper tool for driving
a canoe up a rapid was a setting pole, so I had equipped myself
with one — by chopping down a small spruce and lopping off
the branches with an ax. I had even practiced with this crude
pole a bit in still water. But the river was fast, black, and choppy,
flecked with whitecaps, and I got into trouble almost at once.

To a rank beginner, the most daunting aspect of poling a
canoe is that you have to stand up to do it. Then there is the
problem of steering, which is tricky for a novice even in perfectly calm water, and in a rapid the canoe seems to have a mind
of its own. Try as I might, I could not make the boat go in a
straight line. I zigzagged up the river instead, and as soon as I
encountered the first stretch of really fast water, the bow began
to swing to the right irresistibly. In an instant the canoe was
sideways. It began to tip, slopping water over the gunwale, and
I sat down with a crash, grabbing for the paddle. The canoe was
racing downstream. The best I could do was to slow its descent
a little and try to avoid striking rocks.

Yet a canoe can be poled up rapids much more difficult than
this one if the technique is mastered. The key is finesse, not
brute strength, the main idea being to keep the canoe pointed
directly into the current — to split it with the bow — so that the
current is pressing against the absolute minimum amount of
hull surface. A canoe that is broadside to the current is out of
control, but a canoe facing the current presents a superbly

25

streamlined shape to the moving water — like an alewife. Once the correct alignment is achieved and the end of the pole securely lodged on the riverbed, it takes only a small amount of pressure to hold your position, even in the fastest water. A little more pressure on the pole and you move forward. It is astonishing how well it works.

The bow, however, does not stay lined up of its own accord. Its natural inclination is to fall off to one side or the other. The poler cannot prevent this from happening (since he breaks contact with the riverbed each time he replants the pole), but he can correct the deviation, and it is to his advantage to do so as soon as possible, since for each degree that the bow swings, it exposes that much more hull area for the current to press against. Once the bow swings beyond a certain point, depending on the speed of the current, it is impossible to bring it back, and the canoe is headed for disaster; it is much better to nip this in the bud. Successful poling involves a continual series of minute course corrections best accomplished through delicate shifts of balance and subtle pressures on the pole; if the poler is lunging and grunting he isn't doing it right, and the only way to learn is by practice. The technique has to be automatic. There is no time to think about what is happening in a rapid.

Poling is further complicated by the behavior of the water itself. Rapids run in complex currents of varying strengths that merge and split apart as they swirl around boulders and respond to irregularities in the riverbed, flowing across at different angles, forming eddies and perhaps back currents that may actually flow upstream. The poler has to be able to read the water at a glance. Above all else, he has to stay calm, which is much harder than it sounds. The fear of rapids, I believe, is almost instinctive — and not at all unwarranted. The current can take a metal canoe and bend it around a boulder like a pretzel. Poling demands composure, and I didn't have much of it on that first stab at Enfield Rapids. I was lucky not to fall out of the boat.

But even at the time I didn't feel too bad about my defeat. Enfield Rapids have stymied many a traveler. Adrian Block was forced to turn back here in 1614. The first steamboat to attempt an ascent, a shallow-draft sternwheeler named *Barnet*, was stopped dead in the water on her initial try in November 1826. It was only after the captain had two scows lashed to his vessel, one on either side, each scow crewed by fifteen muscular fallsmen with long setting poles, that the little steamboat made it to the head of the rapids, taking an entire day to cover the 6 miles. *Barnet* eventually went up the river all the way to Bellows Falls, Vermont.

Flatboats propelled by poles and sails were the main type of commercial craft used on the upper Connecticut River. Canals to take them around the rapids above Enfield were built as early as 1795, and the Windsor Locks Canal was finished in 1829. Its completion also allowed regular steamboat service between Hartford and Springfield, although the vessels on this run were no match for the grand sidewheelers on the lower Connecticut. The upriver boats were small, almost like toys, because they had to scoot over sandbars and squeeze into narrow locks. Channel improvements were proposed, but the plans were put aside in 1844, when the railroad was extended from Hartford to Springfield and all commercial navigation on the upper river came to an end.

My train, a single, self-propelled Amtrak diesel car, was arriving. Aside from myself, nobody else got on or off. I bought a ticket from the conductor and braced myself in the aisle as the little train accelerated sharply, roaring like a city bus. The car appeared to be brand new, with beige rugs on the walls, tinted plastic windows, and airplane-style seats with tray tables. There were a dozen other passengers on board. We zipped through downtown Windsor Locks, beside the canal, and in a few minutes were in the woods, bouncing and swaying on an uneven roadbed. A mile or two later the track curved sharply to the right, crossing the canal and the Connecticut River on a long bridge. The rapids were brown and creamy in the bright sunlight.

The first bridge at this site, a covered wooden truss span, blew off its piers in a high wind shortly after the railroad was built. Once on the east bank, the track stays close to the river all the way to Springfield. Now and then I caught glimpses of whitewater through the trees, and we soon passed Enfield Dam and the head of the canal, then flashed by the burned shell of the old Enfield depot, with the ruins of the vast Bigelow carpet mills in the background. Flocks of pigeons swirled through the broken windows. The center of the U.S. carpet industry has long since shifted south, from New England to Dalton, Georgia.

The train ran smoothly now, on jointless welded rail, and the river was placid. A slight bend gave a long view upstream to the distinctive profile of the notch between Mount Tom and Mount Holyoke. The whistle blared for grade crossings as we raced by plowed fields and tobacco barns. I like trains. I always have. When I was twelve years old, my idea of the perfect Saturday afternoon was a train ride from Hartford to Springfield. The New Haven Railroad owned the line in those days, and I remember the dusty blue plush seats in the coaches and the Union News Company vendors — who all seemed to look like Jimmy Durante — walking up and down the aisles with their gray metal baskets. In my eyes everything about the railroad was serious and grown up. It was big and noisy and dirty and steeped in holy ritual. There was a monumental station in Springfield, serving the Boston & Maine and the mighty New York Central (as well as the New Haven), although even in 1958 the cavernous waiting room was often as quiet and empty as a mausoleum. I hung around the tracks, sketching pieces of equipment in my notebook and hoping to be invited up into the cab of a locomotive for a ride. Even better was a visit to the brick signal tower that regulated all train movements. It had an elaborate track diagram with colored lights, like the control panel of some fantastic model railroad, and I used to sit there by the hour, totally absorbed, as trains appeared outside from every direction. When a long freight rumbled across the big steel Connecticut River bridge, the window glass in the tower would rattle. The entire building trembled on its foundation.

Now, as the one-car train pulled into Springfield, I saw that the signal tower was still in use but that its pointed, pagoda-style tile roof had been sliced off by the I-91 overpass. Most of the platform tracks in the station had been torn up, and the old waiting room was closed, replaced by a tiny underground facility in the former pedestrian subway. There was nothing there I wanted to look at. A train for Windsor Locks left ten minutes later, and when I got back to the car, I drove up the east side of the river to the Enfield Dam.

The dam itself, which is only about 9 feet high, was almost completely invisible beneath the heavy flow of water that poured over the lip. The Atlantic salmon runs had already ended before this dam was built, but I would imagine the salmon could have surmounted the low spillway without much difficulty. Shad, on the other hand, had a hard time of it, and the dam was consequently a favorite fishing spot. Steamboat captains coming downstream from Springfield occasionally chose to run Enfield Rapids (to avoid paying the canal toll); Charles Dickens was a passenger on one such trip in 1842. It was February, and the river was full of drifting ice. "I am afraid to tell you," Dickens wrote, "how many feet short this vessel was or how narrow . . . but I may state that we all kept to the middle of the deck lest the boat should suddenly tip over."

Today the dam is broken in several places, making it easier on the shad (and sending anglers elsewhere), but the alewives still seem to have all they can handle. I sat on a big red rock and watched them straining against the current, quivering with effort, almost vibrating as they inched forward only to be swept back down, milling around in the slack water of the eddies, gathering strength to try again. A cool breeze blew off the river. The water was brown and turbulent below the dam, smooth and slick above it. The longer I stared at the broken places in the lip, the more it looked as if it might be possible to run them in a canoe, although I did not have the slightest intention of trying. Perhaps you *could* shoot one of the gaps, but surviving the seething maelstrom at the bottom of the drop would be another matter. Whenever a substantial mass of water plunges down a steep grade, it creates a boiling depression known as a souse hole. A canoe that swamps in a big souse hole is often trapped there, rolling over and over, battering itself into a shapeless pulp, all chance of escape cut off by the inevitable "keeper" wave that breaks upstream, continually trying to fill in the hollow pounded out by the falling water.

The sharpest natural drop in the riverbed at Enfield is about a quarter-mile downstream from the dam, as I discovered in September 1983, when I finally felt confident enough to pole the canoe up the rapids. The first 4 miles from Windsor Locks went quickly enough, but then came a zone of flickering waves. As the current gathered speed I began to lose the bottom. The end of the pole (I had a good pole now, turned on a lathe) wouldn't stick to anything, the bottom being a sheet of red sandstone, smooth as a hardwood floor except for an occasional crack and a number of small potholes. I had to feel for them, and the places where the bottom was the smoothest were also, quite naturally, where the current was the strongest. The sheets of rock extended all the way across the river in a series of broad ledges, like a gradual staircase, each step a few inches high. This was the heart of the rapids. I had never seen such a poor bottom for poling. Time and again I lost my grip, the butt of the pole skidding ineffectually across the polished rock as the canoe began to yaw, but I kept at it, trying different routes, resting whenever I found a solid hold, and at last entered an area of shallow, relatively quiet water where the bottom was sandy, with a thick growth of weeds.

Suddenly a gigantic fish shot underneath the canoe. It must have been at least 4, perhaps 5 feet long, fat across the back with large, coarse scales. I thought it might be a carp, for I had heard stories about huge carp in the Connecticut for years, and during the next few minutes I saw five more of these fabled monsters. Fish are partial to rapids. The steady current brings them a never-ending supply of food. Birds like rapids because of the fish. While I was watching the carp (if that's what they were), an osprey soared overhead. A cormorant sat on a nearby rock, and six mergansers crowded onto another while a great blue heron waded in the shallows. The same kind of good fishing has always drawn men to rapids. Paleo-Indian campsites have been unearthed at several Connecticut River rapids, and pictographs have been found on the rocks. By the nineteenth century, however, the big rapids had become more valuable for their water power than their fish. Dams were built and factories crowded down to the banks, but the Enfield Rapids escaped intensive development because the vertical drop is minor and spread over a long distance, and the rapids here retain a timeless, primitive quality to this day. Or so it seems from a canoe. The sound of the rushing water drowns out all other noises, and the shores are heavily wooded. It is possible to ignore the deep suburbia that lays just beyond, although I find that I like to think of the big malls and the rolling subdivisions. They make the rapids seem that much more precious.

Considerably less water was coming over the top of the dam now than in the spring. The average flow here is 16,470 cubic feet per second, with a recorded low of 1,060 and a high of 280,000. The dam has sagged so far out of true that many spots along the lip were completely dry. I could have put the canoe right up next to it and hopped out without getting my feet wet. The low flow also afforded an opportunity to examine the dam's construction, which appeared to be nothing more elaborate than large stones in a framework of heavy timbers. It was patched here and there with pieces of rusty metal, but if more substantial repairs are not begun soon, the whole thing is going to wash out. Of course, all dams are ultimately doomed to break. In the face of the river's irresistible will, there is no such thing as an immovable object.

3   SPRINGFIELD

to HOLYOKE

Castor canadensis, and Other Dam Builders

THE RECREATIONAL CANOES so common through-
out North America today are direct descendants of the Indian
bark canoe, and although materials have changed for the better
as far as durability is concerned, the basic design is still the
same. It could hardly be improved upon. Few things invented
by the human mind come so close to perfection as a well-made
canoe.

The original bark canoe was largely restricted to the northern boreal forest, a region that encompasses most of what is
now eastern and central Canada as well as Maine, northern
Minnesota, and other border areas, including the northern part
of the Connecticut River watershed. Elsewhere the humble dugout canoe was the typical Indian craft. Dugouts served well as
utility boats and were not nearly so fragile as the lightweight,
thin-skinned bark canoes, but for long-distance wilderness

travel on fast rivers, stormy lakes, and across difficult portages, the bark canoe had no rival. White explorers appreciated this early on and soon put the canoes (and their Indian paddlers) to profitable use in the fur trade.

Furs were a great lure, yielding the maximum return for the minimum investment, and in the north it was always the fur traders who came into a piece of country first — before the homesteaders, before the farmers and the millers and the church builders — skimming off the cream and then turning elsewhere. Many an American fortune can be traced back to the lowly beaver. The canoe was crucial because the fur traders tapped thousands of square miles of otherwise impenetrable territory. Block, however, was just a little before his time. It was a transplanted Englishman named William Pynchon who became the fur king of the Connecticut Valley. In addition to paying off the Indians with goods and trinkets, Pynchon manufactured his own money — wampum — by grinding clamshells into beads and stringing them on lengths of deer gut. Other traders did the same, but few went about it with more energy than Pynchon; he made at least £5,000 worth of the stuff (a fathom of wampum being roughly equivalant to 5 shillings). By 1639 Pynchon had built a warehouse on the east bank of Enfield Rapids to store the furs that came down the river in canoes and were awaiting transfer to oceangoing vessels. In a period of six years he accumulated nine thousand beaver pelts, along with other skins including otter, mink, wolf, fox, fisher, lynx, bobcat, bear, and moose. The place came to be known as Warehouse Point, a name still found on maps today.

The fur trade itself, however, did not last very long. New England was not large enough to provide a continuing supply of pelts, so the fur companies soon turned their attention to Canada and the American West. Pynchon stayed behind and prospered in other commercial ventures. He also earned some distinction as a politician and as a radical theologian. In fact, it was Pynchon's liberal religious views that had first prompted him to leave Boston in 1636 to establish the town of Springfield on the banks of the Connecticut. (Thomas Hooker, the founder of Hartford, left Boston for similar reasons.) Springfield eventually became the largest city in the valley, but its early development seems to have been retarded by the lack of ready access to the outside world. No large ships could pass Enfield Rapids, and overland transportation was primitive in the extreme. Flatboats were used for heavy cargo, but the upriver trip was slow and laborious, and it was not until the eve of the Industrial Revolution that Springfield's population exceeded 3,000 (less than half that of Hartford, and less than that of many other river towns in Connecticut).

The coming of the railroad made the difference. Springfield was fortunate enough to be on one of the first railroads in New England, an east-west route between Boston and Albany that soon became, and still is, the most important line in the region (now owned by Conrail). Springfield matured as a manufacturing center during the nineteenth century, yet even now it seems a lesser city than Hartford, perhaps because Hartford is a state capital or because Springfield, like all cities in Massachusetts, pales in Boston's shadow. Boston has the glamour, Springfield the factories. But if Springfield's riverfront skyline is not so impressive as Hartford's, then neither does Springfield have Hartford's grinding poverty. Despite wealthy suburbs and an immense pool of insurance company capital, Hartford is the fourth poorest city in the United States, according to 1980 census data. Springfield may be a bit drab, but it is a hard-working, solid kind of town.

Unfortunately, this is a matter of some practical concern to a canoeist. I would not consider leaving a car parked unattended at a boat ramp in Hartford. When I drove up to Springfield to launch the canoe on the third of June, I did not give vandalism a second thought. The parking lot by the ramp, which is actually in West Springfield, across the river from downtown, was crowded with cars and boat trailers. A white-haired old fellow with a fishing license pinned to his hat gave me a pretty good going-over as I carried the canoe down to the water. I looked up at him and said, "Nice morning."

"Yup," he said, and then clammed up. It *was* a nice morning, the third one in a row, clear and windless. A pale half moon hung low in the western sky. The river in Springfield did not appear to be any narrower than in Hartford; if anything, the Connecticut seemed wider now. It was exciting. It made me want to hurry. There is always a sense of expectancy when you glide out on the water, and now, as soon as I shoved off, I felt the pull of the current. The river was still high, but without the intense siltiness of the few days before. The water was more green than brown. It was slick and smooth, but not like a lake; it implied hidden power. The sun was hot. Just then a large fish jumped, frozen for an instant in a glittering arc of spray, standing on its tail before it struck the surface of the river with a loud, flat smack. I passed under two bridges: one of them the double-track railroad span by the signal tower, the other, a highway bridge whose heroic concrete arches turned out to be hollow inside; and then the Connecticut stretched out ahead of me, broad and reflective in the harsh urban light. A few grackles and a crow or two picked at flotsam cast up on the bank. I concentrated on paddling, on maintaining a steady rhythm, trying to put my whole body into it, not just the arms.

At some unidentifiable point I passed from Springfield to Chicopee. Springfield, Chicopee, and Holyoke long ago merged into an unbroken industrial-residential corridor, a continuous belt of two-family houses, apartment buildings, abbreviated front yards, madonnas in bathtubs, three-story brick high schools, liquor stores with grilles over the windows; a sprawl of neighborhoods, not downtown and not quite suburb either, the universal zone common to every city in the Northeast since shortly after the beginning of the Industrial Revolution. It was laid out, mainly from scratch, for wagons and trolley cars, then adapted, without complete success, to the automobile, and, like all such places in New England, it has absorbed peoples and cultures like a sponge. During the late nineteenth century, at least thirty different languages were spoken on the streets of Chicopee, with Polish, French, and Italian heard most often. Now Spanish has come on strong. For the last hundred and twenty-five years, neighborhoods like these have been the vital, pumping heart of industrial New England; they still are.

From the river you see the back of Chicopee: roofs through the trees, steeples and smokestacks rising higher, power lines, telephone poles, the blank gaze of abandoned factories, a pair of golden arches, the cinderblock backs of discount stores, big blue dumpsters, bald tires, and shopping carts pushed down a bank. And dikes. A big river is a dangerous and unpredictable neighbor, and men have learned to keep it at arm's length. There is an emotional distance, too, because the river is a thing apart, a thing of motion, a thing defined by motion. Like a freight train in the night, it is always passing through; it does not belong to any one place. But this train never stops. It never holds still. You cannot get a fix on it. It is always different — from one moment to the next — yet it is only doing now what it has always done, what it will always do. There is a raw, primal urgency in the flow, something that seems to hark back to an era when the earth was young, but in truth the river does not belong to any one time any more than it belongs to one place. Its essence, the majestic purposefulness of the flow, its honesty and awesome power, is incorruptible. It can be polluted or dammed, but it cannot be stopped. The river's will cannot be denied. It touches the human soul, and the heart, too, which is good reason to be suspicious of your feelings while out on the water, but I do know this: the reality of the river always surpasses the expectation. Perhaps it will not lead the canoeist to great truths or even to minor ones, but there is always something here to arrest the mind and the eye, and it will bring you back again and again.

By eleven-thirty I had arrived at the mouth of the Chicopee River, which empties into the Connecticut from the east. The Chicopee is the Connecticut's largest tributary, with a watershed of 720 square miles. Quabbin Reservoir, on one of the Chicopee's branches (the Swift River), supplies 40 percent of the drinking water consumed in Massachusetts, including most of Boston's. There seemed to be a goodly amount left over this morning, because the Chicopee was flooding its banks. The current was slack at first, then lively. (The name Chicopee means "rushing water.") About a half-mile in from the mouth, a five-story textile mill loomed beside a set of rapids.

The mill is fairly old, first built in 1843 and then enlarged in 1895, and it is in exceptionally good condition, being almost fully occupied now by retail businesses and small manufacturing concerns. A power canal carries water from the head of the rapids down a long mill yard with narrow, brick buildings on either side. This was the normal layout for textile mills; I suppose you could call it the architecture of running water. Its stamp has been indelibly imprinted on dozens of gritty New England mill towns. The mills were built like fortresses because the machinery was heavy, and they had lots of windows because there were no electric lights. (Hydroelectric generating units did not come into common use until after the turn of the century.) Since the motion of the waterwheels was transmitted by shafts, gears, and leather belts, it was important that the looms and other equipment be as close to the power source as possible. Thus the mills were long and narrow. They were multistoried for the same reason. It was more efficient to stack one floor on top of another than to spread them out over a large area.

Virtually every village in southern New England once had a water mill of some sort. A mill seat, like as not, attracted the settlers in the first place. Today about three thousand mill dams survive in Connecticut alone and perhaps twice that number in Massachusetts, although only a handful still do any useful work. In colonial times the mills ground grain and sawed logs. Enterprising millers soon branched out into the small-scale manufacture of wooden items. A blacksmith usually set up shop nearby, and mill machinery quickly grew more complicated. In an era when draft animals and human muscle were the only alternative sources of power, waterwheels drew tinkerers and inventors like iron filings to a magnet, and by 1840, New England had begun to industrialize in a big way — a development that, among other things, soon rendered water power obsolete.

Nevertheless, water power played a critical role in the early stages of New England's industrial development, particularly in the textile industry, which pioneered in the mass production of inexpensive consumer goods. Spinning and weaving consist of a few simple motions repeated over and over again — exactly the kind of thing that could be done at high speed with the help of falling water. Once the machinery was set up and running it could be tended by a child, and often was. The first New England textile mills were built in the 1790s, and the industry came of age in 1813, when Francis Cabot Lowell built a large and extremely profitable mill in Waltham, near Boston, on the Charles River. Lowell died in 1817, but a group of his original partners, the Boston Associates, built an even bigger mill complex by falls on the Merrimack River, and the Merrimack eventually became the hardest-working mill stream in the world, its waters powering some ninety different textile mills.

Textile mills were scattered throughout the Connecticut River watershed, mainly on tributaries like the Chicopee, but the industry never achieved total dominance here. Connecticut Valley manufacturing was remarkable for its diversity, and there were some interesting local specialties. Westfield, Massachusetts, for example, was known as the Whip City, with seventeen buggy whip factories along the Westfield River, each claiming to produce a superior whip made "the Westfield way." (The West-field River, which rises in the Berkshires, is an important tributary of the Connecticut.) The first gasoline-powered automobile in the United States was driven on the streets of Springfield in 1893, and a sizable tire and auto parts industry later established itself there and in Chicopee. Long before that, however, the Connecticut Valley had become a center of firearms manufacture, with the Springfield Armory, the Colt Works in Hartford, and dozens of smaller companies. Gunmaking was much more complicated than turning out a bolt of gingham cloth, and it quickly led to the invention and use of interchangeable parts, machine tools, and precision measuring devices. Interchangeable parts were of particular importance if you planned to equip an army, and the first government contract to specify this revolutionary feature was awarded to Simeon North of Middletown, Connecticut, in 1813. By 1845, firms such as Robbins & Lawrence in Windsor, Vermont, were turning out high-quality rifles on mechanized production lines for less than $11 each. The New England industrial revolution was working up to speed.

The break from water power was not long in coming. One disadvantage of depending on rivers for power was the uneven rate of flow. Streams flooded in the spring, dried up in the summer, and froze in the winter, but the real problem was one of quantity; there just wasn't enough water power to go around, at least not in the big cities where industrialists wanted to build their plants. Mills turned to stationary steam engines, first as auxiliary power and then as the main power source. The whole story can be traced by looking at the back of the textile mill on the Chicopee River: next to the tail race at the lower end of the canal is a boiler room with a towering smokestack, and next to it is a much newer hydroelectric powerhouse, which was added after the mill's old waterwheels were shut down for good.

I decided to take a stab at ascending the rapids alongside the mill, and the backwash along the flooded banks carried me upstream, almost without any effort on my part, until a band of sharp ledges blocked further progress. Where the river wasn't foaming it was green and glossy, almost black, like bottle glass, and in the sandy-bottomed shallows the water was clear and golden. Sandpipers darted between the waves, peeping, and the eddies were thick with alewives that thumped against the hull of the canoe. I stepped ashore and settled down on a grassy spot in the shade where I could gaze across the river at the mill. The ancient bricks, weathered now to a soft, mournful hue, were made from Connecticut Valley clay. A few of the hundreds of windows that faced the rapids were propped open, and it looked hot inside. Nothing is as hot as a milltown in the summer. My dad used to sell advertising space for a metalworking trade magazine, making calls in every mill town in New England — Athol, Greenfield, Holyoke, Chicopee, the whole dreary lot. I have worked in machine tool factories in Connecticut and Vermont, and I can still feel the sour summer heat, scented with hydraulic fluid and lubricant and flavored with the shriek of metal cutting metal at high speed, honing it down to tolerances measured to the thousandth of an inch while the chips piled up around your greasy work shoes like silver pencil shavings. I met the night watchman at the Chicopee mill once, when I wandered into the mill yard on a hot, absolutely silent Sunday afternoon; we got to talking and I asked him if the canal and powerhouse were still used for anything.

"That's the electric light," he said. For the city." He was a tall Polish man who appeared to be about sixty-five. In fact, he was eighty-two years old, born in 1901. He said that he had gone into the textile mills straight off the boat, in Lowell, Massachusetts, when he was thirteen, working his way up to weaver and quitting when he was twenty-one. He came to Chicopee and got a job in a coal yard, moving later to a track gang on the B&M Railroad, then into a foundry, and finally to the big Westinghouse plant. Now he was a night watchman. It made

him laugh to remember it all, as if it was a faintly amusing practical joke that had been played on someone he didn't know too
well. It was the same way I finally came to feel about my army
tour in Vietnam.

Some high, puffy clouds had appeared in the sky; the wind
would be picking up soon. I got back in the canoe and shoved
off, riding the swift, bouncy current of the rapids to the smooth
water below. A pair of fancy bass boats had nosed into the
mouth of the Chicopee River, their owners sitting in the ele-
vated fishing chairs while little electric trolling motors churned
away quietly. I headed up the Connecticut, past a boat ramp and
under some power lines and the Mass. Pike bridge. A flood dike
ran along the east bank. Bluffs rose in the west.

After a while the river curved around a sharp bend to the
east, and the first of the vast Holyoke mills appeared on the left.
I had been using the motor for the past half-hour because of a
bothersome headwind, and now the current began to assert itself with a vengeance. There is a major set of rapids — Hadley
Falls — about a mile and a half upstream. Before the great Holyoke dam was built in 1848, the Hadley Falls rapids were about
6 miles long, with the greater portion of the 53-foot vertical drop
concentrated in a short stretch of violent whitewater. The dam
has drowned the upper section, and during conditions of normal flow, most of the impounded water is diverted into Holyoke's multilevel industrial canal system, leaving the riverbed
dry immediately below the dam. In the spring, however, excess
water is released to flow down its old course, and the rapids
suggest some of their former glory.

The river was full now. It stretched out straight in front of
me, then swung to the north in another sharp curve; even if I
had not known that the rapids were just around the bend, I
might have inferred it from the lay of the land. A range of rocky
hills blocks the valley here, and the river has no choice but to
slice through them, a situation that is almost guaranteed to pro-

duce a sharp drop in the riverbed. The passage is most dramatic a few miles upstream, where the river, after meandering placidly across a flat floodplain, abruptly dives into a narrow slot in the mountains not unlike the Middletown Narrows.

The sight could be saved for another day. I wasn't sure I could even make it up to the dam, since the current seemed to be getting stronger by the minute. As I passed under a railroad bridge, the racing water foamed on the pointed upstream edges of the piers like the bow waves on a fleet of stone ships. My forward progress had slowed to an agonizing creep. The straining motor sounded ready to tear itself apart. In the meantime, other boats were roaring up and down the river, passing me as if I were standing still, rocking me with their 80-horsepower wakes. I began to notice clusters of fishermen standing along the banks, and when I finally swung around the curve, I saw where all the power boats had been going. There were at least three dozen of them anchored out in the current, fishing. Another fifty or sixty fishermen were dangling lines off the highway bridge at the foot of the rapids. The great vertical wall of the Holyoke dam loomed in the distance. Water poured over the top and came thundering down the steep, rocky riverbed in a creamy torrent.

The fishermen were after shad, of course, and though I saw a couple of big fish jump, I could not find anybody who had caught one. The local wisdom seemed to be that the run was just about over, but if there were fish to be found anywhere, this was the place. Shad tend to congregate here before ascending the rapids and wear themselves out in futile attempts to jump over the dam. Eventually they flop down on the dam's concrete apron, totally exhausted, and most find their way into the fish elevator, along with alewives, blueback herring, and perhaps even an Atlantic salmon or two. The Connecticut River salmon restoration project, in progress for eighteen years, is beginning to show results. The first returning salmon was spotted in 1975. In 1981, 530 returning salmon were captured. About 300,000 shad now ride the Holyoke fish elevator each spring.

In the old days, the flatboat traffic above and below Hadley Falls was heavy enough to warrant the construction of a navigation canal, in 1795, on the east side of the rapids. It had one unusual feature: boats were floated onto a movable device, which was then pulled up an incline on a cable powered by a waterwheel. The incline was later replaced by a set of five conventional locks. For most of the period that the canal was in use, only a few small wing dams served to retard the Connecticut at Hadley Falls. The city of Holyoke did not exist at all. It was built during the mid-nineteenth century, in conjunction with the big dam, as a planned industrial community. The attraction, obviously, was water power; it was the greatest single water power source anywhere in southern New England, and Holyoke today, with its mills and canals, is a monument to that era, well worth getting out of the canoe for a closer look.

4 ☙ HOLYOKE

to NORTHAMPTON

Time and the River

*H*OLYOKE, Massachusetts. No other city in the Connecticut Valley gives so vivid a picture of nineteenth-century industrial America. Holyoke is pure New England mill town. For the best effect the view should be from the east, from the top of a bluff, on a raw morning when the scudding clouds are the color of an old Salvation Army overcoat. First there is the river, wide and full of rapids, swinging around a curve, and then the city itself, climbing the hills on the far bank. Holyoke is vast, dense, and somber. Cold black water races through the canals. Smokestacks and church spires reach into the sky. There are bricks, millions upon millions of dark, sooty bricks, and a wealth of detail: granite windowsills, brass weathervanes, copper-sheathed cupolas, bell towers, ornamental ironwork, heavy wooden doors, cobblestone alleys, stone steps worn smooth by millworkers' feet. Holyoke was built for the ages. The mill buildings, even in abandonment, are awesome. The architecture was meant to intimidate. The winter wind never blows colder than it does down these bleak streets lined with rusting cars, three-decker wooden houses, and brick tenement blocks. The bars fill up at eight in the morning. The unemployment offices are crowded.

The present Holyoke Water Power Company dam is a large, surprisingly graceful structure about a thousand feet long, but the first dam at this site was an embarrassing failure. It collapsed during the dedication ceremony in 1848, washing down the river before the astonished eyes of the assembled dignitaries. The dam was rebuilt, but twenty-four of the original twenty-five cotton mill sites beside the canal system remained vacant, and the Hadley Falls Company slid into bankruptcy. Holyoke's major product eventually turned out to be paper, not textiles. Now the Holyoke paper industry has faded, but the dam still generates electricity. When I inspected the facility in April 1983, the powerhouse was being enlarged so that an additional set of turbines and generators could be installed. A pair of colossal penstocks — concrete pipes big enough to drive a dump truck through — led down from the dam, and one of them had been opened. There were men inside it, working.

I crossed over to the east side of the Connecticut and found a place to launch the canoe near a small bicentennial park that commemorates the old Hadley Falls navigation canal. A short section of the canal has been restored to an approximation of its nineteenth-century appearance. Despite the restraining influence of the dam, just a half-mile downstream, there was a substantial current running in the river, this being the peak of the runoff. There was a stiff wind also, blowing upstream for once. It raised a chop in the silty brown water, but with the wind at my back, the canoe was rock steady. Mount Tom loomed in the distance where the river made a turn to the right. According to the diagram on a brass plaque in the park, the old canal ended at about that point, and there was a low dam, like the one at

Enfield, reaching all the way across to the opposite shore. It was just high enough to smooth out the last bit of whitewater.

The dam has been gone for years, and as I approached the bend under Mount Tom I felt the current accelerate. I could see it accelerate. The surface of the water had a tight, tense look to it, like metal subjected to extreme stress. Out in the middle of the river a large tree shot by, rolling over and over. I stayed close to the bank. Outside of an actual rapid, I do not believe I have ever seen a current this powerful. There was no way my little 2-horsepower motor could make any headway against it. If the current started to drive me down the river stern first or if the motor suddenly quit, the canoe would probably swing around broadside and swamp; I wasn't sure what to do. I deliberated for a bit and decided to set the bow at a forty-five-degree angle to the flow so that the force of the current pressing against the hull, combined with the forward thrust of the motor, would ferry the canoe across the river to the west shore. It worked perfectly, and once on the other side I found a convenient back current, just as I thought I might. It petered out all too soon, but the river was flooding the woods a little (something it hadn't been able to do on the east shore because of sheer rock banks), and the water among the trees was relatively quiet and shallow enough to use the setting pole. It was easy going. After a while I came to some broad ledges of dark red stone that jutted out into the main current, raising a formidable set of standing waves. I tied the canoe to a tree and got out to look for dinosaur tracks.

The ledges ran into the river on a slant, the rock laid down in thin, flat plates in dozens of layers, something like sheets of mica. Where the top layers had flaked away it revealed sets of wavy ripple marks that resembled the ripples in the mud of a shallow lake bottom, which is exactly what they were: fossilized ripples about 100 million years old. Fossil-bearing rocks such as these are prime territory for dinosaur tracks, and with that in mind, it becomes difficult to keep from seeing, or imagining that you see, them everywhere. Every irregularity in the rock begins to look like a track. The best tracks at this particular location, however, are a bit farther inland, on unweathered slabs exposed during highway construction.

I crossed the B&M Railroad and followed a short path through the woods to a tilted sheet of red rock beneath the U.S. 5 retaining wall. If I thought I had been seeing tracks before, I knew I was seeing them now. Some looked fresh enough to have been made last week. It was eerie. The slab was covered with clear, sharp tracks in three distinct sizes — small, large, and huge — all of them three-toed, like the footprints of giant birds. The largest tracks, made by a predatory dinosaur that walked upright on its hind legs and stood about 12 feet tall, were an inch deep and long enough to contain one of my bulky, size nine insulated shoe pacs with plenty of room left over.

It wasn't so much the size of the tracks that got to me as their great age. How can a man who might live to be seventy-five or eighty, if he's lucky, even begin to deal with something that has endured more than 100 million years, especially something as lifelike as these footprints? The dinosaur that made them, moreover, had quite plainly been going somewhere. Six or seven of his big tracks went in a line across the slab. I assume he wasn't in much of a hurry because by stretching my legs I was able to match his stride. I could see where mud had squished up around his toes. It was easy to imagine his great weight pressing down into the ground, the soft mud making sucking noises as he lifted his feet. I could almost see the great thick legs, heavily muscled, and the large head with the keen eyes shaded by ridges of supraorbital bone, like an eagle's. Then I heard a train coming. A blue diesel locomotive rumbled by with a string of empty coal cars, and the dinosaur was gone.

Since about 1850, thousands of dinosaur tracks have been discovered in the Connecticut Valley, and they were instrumental in forming our early impressions of what dinosaurs were like. But there is a limit to how much you can learn about an animal from its tracks, and as fossilized bones and skeletons began to turn up in other parts of the country, the attention of paleontologists shifted away from New England. The current hot spots of American dinosaur paleontology are in the dry canyonlands of Utah and Colorado, and a major reevaluation of the dinosaurs is now in progress. The popular conception of dinosaurs as pea-brained behemoths wallowing in primordial ooze is not entirely obsolete, but it has been expanded to include dinosaurs with acute senses, keen reflexes, a high degree of mobility, and complicated patterns of social behavior. Some dinosaurs may have been warm-blooded. Had it not been for a global extermination caused by an unknown catastrophic event at the close of the Mesozoic Era, the dinosaurs might have evolved into some sort of intelligent, manlike creature. But the dinosaur line is not completely extinguished; the birds are their descendants.

As the tracks by the Connecticut River suggest, many dinosaurs were fairly small, but I found myself wondering about their gigantic cousins, the great, long-necked vegetarians that browsed placidly on the upper branches of the ancient coniferous forests. What sort of noises did those gentle colossi make? Surely they were not mute. Big gizzard stones may have rumbled in their multiple stomachs, and some paleontologists believe that dinosaurs could sing. But what sort of songs? Did 50-ton divas take parts in titanic, reptilian operas? By and large, however, Mesozoic Massachusetts must have been quiet, as all great wildernesses are quiet. It was quiet for an eternity, for several eternities. The Mesozoic Era — the age of reptiles — began 230 million years ago, and it stretched on and on for 165 million years. There was more than enough time for the entire cycle of Western civilization — exploration, Indian wars, industrialization, and nuclear holocaust — to be played over and over again, like a recorded telephone message, but of course it was not. The dinosaurs were the lords of the earth, and they went about their business unperturbed. Then they disappeared, and the Cenozoic Era began. It has lasted 65 million years, so far.

A far greater span stretches backward from the Mesozoic, back into the Paleozoic Era, which lasted 345 million years, and on back into the fathomless, 4,000-million-year depths of Precambrian time. About midway through the Paleozoic Era all the land masses on the planet began to draw together to form the supercontinent of Panagea, a drawn-out process that continued until the start of the Mesozoic Era. Then, about 140 million years ago, Panagea began to break apart. The movement was exceedingly slow at first, but it became more rapid as the supercontinent divided into northern and southern halves — Laurussian and Gondwana — and split down the middle to create the beginning of the Atlantic Ocean. About 120 million years ago, the attendant strains in the earth's crust caused a hundred-mile-long rift valley to tear open in central New England. Volcanic activity followed, sometimes explosively, more often with lava welling up to form dikes. In the meantime, rivers and streams were wearing down the surrounding landscape, and the resulting sediment was deposited on the valley floor, where it spread out in flat sheets. Dinosaurs walked in the mud and left tracks. Ripple marks formed on the bottom of shallow pools. As the mud dried, it oxidized to a deep red color and was compressed into rock — Triassic redbeds — as more layers built up on top. Eventually the rift valley filled with sedimentary rock, but it did not disappear entirely because the infant Connecticut River had selected this great trench as its course and had already begun to reexcavate it.

After millions of years of erosion, the general outline of the valley can still be seen today. The river flows through it from Greenfield, Massachusetts, to Middletown, Connecticut (and once followed the valley all the way to New Haven until a course change set the lowermost river flowing southeast to Old

Saybrook). Lava dikes have long since been uncovered to form traprock cliffs, and "new" dinosaur tracks keep turning up at construction sites. The valley's distinguishing feature, the Triassic redbeds, are everywhere: in ledges, outcroppings, boulders, sand, and dirt. The soft, handsome rock has been used locally for everything from bridge piers to headstones, and it has been exported as far away as California. Most of the brownstone houses in New York City are faced with rock quarried along the river near Middletown and Portland. The redbeds, like the mill towns and the tobacco fields, give the valley a strong sense of place.

❧

As you face upstream, Mount Tom rises from the left side of the river, Mount Holyoke from the right, and it is only after passing through this gap that the true scale of the ancient valley is fully revealed. Suddenly the landscape is flat and the Connecticut meanders across a broad, fertile floodplain in lazy loops. Rivers do not like to flow in straight lines. They will seldom do so for a distance greater than ten times the width of their channel. Meandering (a term that can be traced to the Maiandros River in Turkey) is most pronounced in mature rivers with level floodplains and easily worked alluvial soils. The process is simple. Once a slight curve is started, material is removed from the outside of the curve (where the current is strongest) and carried downstream to be deposited on a bar or on the inside of another curve. Curves are usually initiated by solid objects that protrude into the channel, deflecting the flow, but a river will form meanders in the absence of any noticeable obstacles. The curves, moreover, have a characteristic shape. According to Luna Leopold and W. B. Langbein, "a given series of meanders tends to have a constant ratio between the wavelength of the curve and the radius of the curvature." Leopold and Langbein called this a "sine-generated curve," stating that it "differs from a sine curve, from a series of connected semicircles, or from any other familiar geometric curve in that it has the smallest variation of the changes in direction." A meander assumes the shape of a sine-generated curve because it is the path that requires the least work in turning.

The formation and enlargement of curves are continual processes, and given enough time, the channel will occupy every conceivable position between one edge of the valley and the other. If you could watch a movie of the river taken by a time-lapse camera over several thousand years, the channel would wiggle across the floodplain like a snake. Substantial changes in course, however, are sometimes observable within the span of a human lifetime. It is also quite easy to trace the courses that have been abandoned by a meandering river, especially if you look down on the valley floor from a height. Old meander loops are occasionally preserved as oxbow lakes, the best example in the Connecticut Valley being directly beneath the north slope of Mount Tom in Northampton, Massachusetts. The Northampton oxbow was cut off from the river in 1830.

Unlike the meandering of a river, most changes in the landscape are so slow as to be imperceptible, and, partly because of this, men did not begin to appreciate the incredible amounts of time involved until relatively recently. For most of recorded history a biblical time scale was accepted. The earth was thought to be about 5,000 years old, and the way the land looked in, say, the year 1550 was thought to be the way it had always looked. Anomalies such as marine fossils in the Alps or glacial moraines in England were explained by Noah's flood. There was little appreciation of the slow-motion majesty of the geologic process — or even that a geologic process existed. Gradually, however, the frontiers of deep time were pushed back. In 1785, James Hutton published his *Theory of the Earth*, in which he stated that in regard to the age of the planet, "we find no vestige of a beginning, no prospect of an end." The first university geology course was taught at about the same time, from 1781 to 1803. Then Louis Agassiz (1807–1873) studied living glaciers in Switzerland and old moraines in Massachusetts, making doubters believe that there had been ice ages in times past. If half the North American continent could once have been covered by ice a mile thick — a preposterous idea on the face of it — then what other wonders were possible? The existence of dinosaurs for one, and Darwin's theory of natural selection for another. Both require a very old earth to be plausible.

Alfred Wegener, a German who, like Agassiz, had a deep interest in glaciology, put forward an even more astounding theory, that the continents themselves were in motion, drifting about the globe to bump into each other and then split apart again. It is only during the last two decades that plate tectonics — continental drift — has won widespread acceptance among geologists; and their reluctance was natural, considering that Wegener's version of earth history stood geology on its head. But plate tectonics also made this history a good deal more understandable. Take mountains, for example. Before plate tectonics, there was no real explanation for mountain building. The structure of mountains was well understood, as were the processes of erosion and sedimentation, but what actually raised the mountains up in the first place was a mystery. To quote Professor James Dana of Yale, geologists had "a theory of the origin of mountains with the origin of mountains left out." Drifting continents provide an answer. In the case of New England, most (but not all) of the mountains originally arose as a result of the immense forces generated during the collision of plates that formed Panagea.

It did not happen quickly, and as soon as the mountains began to rise, running water began to tear them down. This is the endless contest: erosion versus uplift. Many of the original ranges were worn down to nubs, only to be raised again and worn down once more. But as ancient as the New England mountains may seem (and the basement rocks in the Green Mountains of Vermont are 700 million years old, those in the Adirondacks older still), they represent only a recent chapter of earth history. The planet itself is 4,600 million years old. If you divide that span into a single twelve-month year, then Panagea began to form about the middle of November. It was complete by December 13 or 14, slightly before the dinosaurs first appeared, and it began to split apart on the twentieth. The dinosaurs were extinct two days later, but primitive mammals had already established themselves. Man appeared late in the day on December 31 (5 million years ago), and he learned how to read and write partway through the last second before midnight.

సౌ

The first men to set foot in North America came from Siberia across the Bering Land Bridge at some point during the Ice Age, perhaps 50,000 years ago, perhaps much more recently. They spread out to the south and east, and some of their descendants arrived in the Connecticut Valley about 10,000 years ago, as the ice sheet was slowly melting. Archaeologists have since dubbed these people the Paleo-Indians, but not a great deal is known about them, aside from some elegantly crafted fluted spear points and a few other tools that have been unearthed at a dozen or so campsites. There were never very many Paleo-Indians, and they were highly nomadic, following the mammoths and the great herds of caribou that roamed the postglacial tundra of New England. As the climate gradually warmed and the forestland increased, the Paleo-Indians moved farther north, on the heels of the retreating glaciers.

Some of the Paleo-Indians may have stayed behind, but they soon mingled with subsequent waves of Indian immigrants who came to New England from the Midwest, from the Great Lakes and the Ohio Valley. The new arrivals introduced corn to New England, along with such crops as pumpkins, squash, and beans, among other things, but while agriculture became an important part of New England Indian life, it did not eclipse hunting. The Indians kept no domestic animals except dogs, and cultivation of the soil was women's work, although the men did tend some plots of tobacco. The total amount of land under cultivation was never very great.

In fact, there were not many Indians in New England, perhaps 100,000 at the most, and their numbers were continually whittled away (to about 18,000 by the 1630s) by epidemics and wars. The tribes of the lower Connecticut Valley were generally small and weak, and they were mercilessly harassed by formidable enemies — the Abnakis to the north, the Narragansetts to the east, the Montauks to the south, and, most feared of all, the Mahicans to the west. In later years, a group of Mahicans migrated to eastern Connecticut, where they became known as the Pequots; the name meant "destroyer" in the Algonquin language.

Then the white man arrived, and things got worse. To be fair, many of the colonists tried to be honest in dealing with the Indians, at least in the beginning. This contract between John Pynchon (William Pynchon's son) and the Connecticut Valley Indians of central Massachusetts is fairly typical:

> Be it known to all men by these presents that Chickwollop alias Wahillowa, Umpanchala alis Womscom, and Quomquont alias Wompshaw, the sachems on Nolwotogg, the sole and proper owners of all the land on the east side of the Quonicticot River do give, grant, bargin and sell unto John Pynchon of Springfield, his assigns and succesors forever, all the grounds, woods, ponds, waters, meadows, trees, stones, etc., lying on the east side of the Quonictocot River within the compass afresaid for and in consideration of two hundred fathoms of wampum which Chickwollop sets off, besides several small gifts . . . all and singular the aforementioned land, or by whatever name it is or may be called, quietly to have, possess and enjoy the aforesaid tract of land free from all molestation and incumbrances of Indians, and that forever, only the Indians afrementioned doth reserve and keep one corn field, and also they reserve liberty to hunt deer, fowl, etc., and to take fish, beaver, or otter, etc.

But good intentions were beside the point. To see the problem as the Indians did, imagine that a small group of strangers suddenly show up on your doorstep. They don't speak the language and they are cold and hungry, obviously unable to take proper care of themselves in a new environment, so you invite them inside. They are thankful, but also arrogant and condescending. Worst of all, it seems they have no intention of leaving. In fact, they send for their friends and relatives. The house is getting crowded, and before long the strangers insist on buying it, suggesting that you move to a tent in the back yard. The amount of money offered is irrelevant; you have to fight.

The first armed conflict between Indians and whites in the Connecticut Valley erupted in 1634, and shortly afterward the Pequots attacked Wethersfield, Connecticut, killing nine people. The colonists allied themselves with a group of dissident Pequots called the Mohegans and pursued the rest of the Pequot warriors to Mystic, Connecticut, where a massacre took place. The Pequot War was followed by several decades of peace, but then the Wampanoags, led by King Philip, and the Narragansetts began to raid white settlements, and by 1675 the fighting had spread to the Connecticut Valley. Deerfield, Northfield, Springfield, and other towns were burned, and the white settlers suffered heavy casualties, as did the Indians, who lost 5,000, killed or wounded. But King Philip's War, as it came to be known, was over in a year. Canoonchet, the leader of the Narragansetts, was captured in 1676, his head put on public display in Hartford. Philip surrendered that same summer. Most of the Indian survivors fled to New York or Canada.

Yet the Indians (and their new French allies) managed to hinder the settlement of the upper Connecticut Valley for the next eighty-five years. Whenever white people tried to reoccupy northern towns like Deerfield or to build forts farther up the valley, Indian raiding parties swept down from Canada, burning houses and carrying captives off into the woods. These episodes culminated in the French and Indian War of 1755–1763. Actually, there had been three previous French and Indian wars — King William's War (1689–1697), Queen Anne's War (1702–1713), and King George's War (1745–1748) — consisting mainly of skirmishes. In 1763 the English captured Québec and the Indians laid down their arms. The entire Connecticut Valley was safe for the white man.

White settlers went on to change the face of the land, yet an Indian presence still lingers, even though the Indians have been gone for more than two centuries. Corn is still the dominant crop; pumpkins, squash, and tobacco are still grown; maple trees are still tapped in the spring; lacrosse is still played; but the Indian legacy is also felt in subtler, more important ways. When the colonists arrived in the New World they were ignorant of the wilderness. England was a settled country; few Englishmen had ever chopped down a tree or shot at wild game. The Indians taught them how to hunt, how to survive, and much else besides. No doubt the white men would have acquired this knowledge on their own, but they learned the Indian ways, albeit imperfectly, and made them a part of the culture, an essential part of the American character, so they still are today, long after the frontier faded. You sense this every time you get in a canoe, if only in the fuzziest, romantic sort of way. The Indian place names have a stronger magic, the names of rivers most of all: the Chicopee, the Ashuelot, the Ammonoosuc, the Passumpsic, the Nulhegan, and of course the Connecticut itself, the Long River.

5 &. NORTHAMPTON
to TURNERS FALLS

Spectators

THE CONNECTICUT RIVER, like most rivers, is not
as old as the landscape through which it flows. The Connecticut
dates back only to the late Mesozoic Era, to the opening of the
great rift valley, and even then the river did not come to resemble its present form for another 70 or 80 million years. On the
other hand, streams have drained the New England mountains
for as long as the mountains have existed, and some of those
ancient streams can be counted as the Connecticut's distant
ancestors. All streams, moreover, are nourished by the same
fund of water, and the total amount of water on the earth has
remained virtually constant for a long time indeed. There is no
more and no less water today than there was 80 million years
ago — or 800 million years ago. Water is neither created nor
destroyed; it simply moves from one place to another in continual circulation, so, in a sense, every stream is ageless, at once
both old and young.

I once read that a river is "the terrestrial phase of the hydrologic cycle." It is a good reminder that a river is not so much a discrete entity as it is part of a much larger global system, not so much a thing as a process. I am tempted to say that a river is a means to an end, but in the river's case the means *is* the end. Without motion, without process, a river does not exist. The trouble with the hydrologic cycle is that it's so big; it is hard, in fact impossible, to get a look at the whole thing. But you can come a little closer to this goal by seeking out long views, and one of the best is the view from the observation tower on top of North Sugarloaf Mountain in South Deerfield, Massachusetts.

Imagine this: having climbed the spiral staircase you are standing on the tower's open deck, hands on the railing, facing south. The red cliffs of Sugarloaf fall away steeply on three sides, almost like those of a mesa. The Connecticut River is close by, 350 feet below, a broad silver ribbon unwinding in a gradual curve across a floodplain dotted with white villages, tobacco barns, and the odd plastics factory and drive-in movie screen. Tiny cars crawl along the highways that slice through the fields, but the flowing river leads the eye south, to the distant high-rise dormitories of the University of Massachusetts at Amherst and beyond, to the undulating crests of Mount Tom and the Holyoke Range, marching across the horizon like a line of waves frozen into stone. Careful inspection reveals the gap through which the river passes to seek the sea. On either margin of the valley are ancient, waterworn hills, each crease in their flanks created by a tributary stream, and above the hills is a vast dome of sky, alive with water vapor and charged with wind as shafts of sunlight and cloud shadows walk the valley floor. Perhaps there is a hawk rising on a thermal or a rain shower in the distance.

With this much space, and a little imagination, it is possible to sense the wholeness of the hydrologic cycle, of the timeless river itself. It is a view that causes a sharp rush of pleasure every time you look down on it. There is something providential and generous about this great valley, something that touches the heart. A nineteenth-century tourist, Charles Eldridge, described the scene in 1833: "An almost perfect plain extends each side of the river, with every inch of soil cultivated — the ground groaning under the weight of its rich but honest burden, the far brought Connecticut that here lords it in the very lap of luxury, comes sluggishly meandering on a perfect parallel to Hogarth's 'Line of Beauty.'"

Onions were the big crop then, with tobacco gaining ground later. As recently as 1950, Hartford County, Connecticut, ranked twenty-sixth of all the counties in the United States in the value of its agricultural crops, mainly shade tobacco, with Franklin and Hampshire counties in Massachusetts not far behind. Now shade tobacco is gone from the Massachusetts section of the Connecticut Valley, done in by high costs (one acre of shade tobacco requires 5,000 yards of cheesecloth and 350 pounds of wire, plus irrigation and hand labor) and by a much less expensive product called "sheet tobacco" (made from pulverized tobacco plants and used for cigar wrappers, replacing the prime shade leaf). But a little broadleaf tobacco is still grown in the valley, along with onions, potatoes, asparagus, and garden truck. Farm stands offer apples, tomatoes, cider, cheese, maple syrup, pumpkins, squash, sweet corn, and Indian corn. Pick-your-own berry fields are increasingly popular. The Connecticut Valley remains the most productive agricultural region in Massachusetts.

༄

There is a boat ramp in the little town of Sunderland, Massachusetts, just across the Connecticut from North Sugarloaf Mountain, and I launched the canoe there on a bitter cold morning in January 1983. There had been rain and sleet the night before, but now the clouds were disintegrating. Grass rattled in the sharp wind, and branches clicked together nervously; I watched an old newspaper blow across a stubble field. It was a headwind, of course, and too strong to paddle against; I had to use the motor from the start. To judge from a thin residue of ice that ran along the bank like the waterline on a ship, the river had fallen a foot or two sometime in the recent past. Perhaps the dam at Turners Falls was holding water back.

Over on the west side of the river I could see the metal roof of a long, single-story cow barn that belongs to the U. Mass. dairy facility. The University of Massachusetts was once an agricultural college, but it has long since knocked the manure off its shoes. In fact, this whole area doesn't feel much like country anymore. There is a hard, urban edge to the roar of the traffic. Rental housing, indoor tennis courts, and Dansk factory outlets have sprung up in the fields. None of this intrudes upon the river, however. Precious little ever does.

I aimed the canoe behind a wooded island, thinking it might cut the wind, but found shallow water and gravel bars instead. There were ducks on the river, including some paired mallards, and a few gulls, too. The gulls were calm, the ducks jittery, never letting me come close. Refusing to learn by experience, I went behind another island and encountered more shallows, which forced me to get out and wade, pulling the canoe by its painter through the little riffles where the current ran over the bars. Hundreds of clams clung to the smooth gray stones, and the pearly, inner surfaces of the shells were a delicate pink. It was hard to take a step without treading on half a dozen. I was wearing rubber boots, and the water felt no colder than the air. The current pressed against my legs. The clear water flashed transparently in the sun, magnifying and distorting the gravel in the riverbed. The words "terrestrial phase of the hydrologic cycle" kept running through my head.

The amounts of water in the different phases of the hydrologic cycle at any given moment are a bit surprising. Although you would expect the oceans to hold a lot of water, they actually contain even more than you might guess: 95.2 percent. Another 2.8 percent is locked up in glaciers and ice caps. Some 1.9 percent is in rivers, streams, lakes, and groundwater, leaving just 0.1 percent to circulate through the atmosphere. Rainfall, moreover, is unevenly distributed around the globe, although southern New England gets a goodly share, about 45 inches per year. Most people, I suspect, would say that it rains too much. In the summer, the Connecticut Valley can seem like a steamy green jungle. Thick fogs rise off the river in the morning, and in the afternoon the sky is white with milky heat haze. Vegetation takes hold everywhere. Weeds can overrun a vacant lot or a railroad yard in no time at all. Farmers have come to expect two or three good hay crops a season, and they have to keep an eye peeled for sudden thunderstorms while mowing.

Irrigation, by far the major water use in the United States, is negligible in New England. It simply isn't necessary except for a few crops like tobacco, and cities here do not have to compete with agriculture for water, as they do in the arid Southwest. Nevertheless, New England metropolitan areas still manage to experience drinking water shortages. The problem is not new; when Boston began running into trouble in the early years of the twentieth century, it took the radical step of pirating water from the Connecticut River drainage basin. A dam was built on the Swift River, a tributary of the Chicopee, and the resulting reservoir — Quabbin — sits up in the hills 12 miles due west of Sunderland. It is the largest body of water in the Connecticut River watershed, the third largest in New England.

Quabbin was an ambitious construction project for the 1930s; it would be a big project in any era. Four entire townships in the Swift River valley — Dana, Enfield, Greenwich, and Prescott — had to be dismantled. Houses, stores, churches, mills, and barns were demolished or moved. Graveyards were dug up and relocated. All the timber was cut and hauled off or heaped into piles and burned. The dam and aqueducts were completed in 1939 and the water began to rise, spreading over the plucked landscape, probing into side valleys to form bays and inlets. By 1946 the reservoir was full.

Now the scars have healed. Quabbin has become a virtual wilderness, albeit an intensively managed wilderness with lots of rules. Fishing is allowed, as are small outboard motors. Sailing, swimming, snowmobiling, cross-country skiing, hunting, and camping are prohibited. There are hiking trails, and bird watching is extremely popular. The area provides a refuge for all sorts of wildlife — perhaps even mountain lions — and it has a winter population of bald eagles. There is nothing else quite like Quabbin in southern New England.

The eagles were what stirred my imagination, and they prompted Linda Hay and me to drive down to Quabbin on a brisk day in March 1982. Following the instructions of a woman in the administration building who was used to eagle watchers, we took a winding road up into the hills to a pullout overlooking the basin. Six other cars were there already, parked next to spotting scopes set up on tripods. The frozen reservoir was spread out far below us like a map, and wave after wave of snowy, rounded ridgetops reached out toward the Berkshires in the west, with the Connecticut Valley concealed in one of the folds. I turned off the ignition and felt a gust of wind rock the car on its springs. A red-faced man in a blue down parka got out of a Chevy Blazer and invited me to use his spotting scope, but when I squatted down behind the eyepiece I couldn't see a thing. A high-power spotting scope takes some getting used to. My eyes adjusted gradually, and a group of blurry objects that I had taken for rocks came into focus, sprouting heads and legs. They were deer, almost a mile away, browsing by the edge of the reservoir. Heat waves shimmered above the ice. There were no eagles.

After teetering on the brink of extinction for decades, eagles have begun a tentative comeback. The summer population of bald eagles in the United States — excluding Alaska — is now about three thousand birds, with additional eagles visiting in the winter. The Quabbin eagles, some fifteen to thirty of them, come from Maine and eastern Canada. They feed on winterkill deer and whatever else is available. I suspect that Quabbin's solitude is a big attraction, too. The closest I have ever been to a wild eagle was on an 11,000-foot mountain in Idaho. I was spending the night on the summit, and as the sun began to go down, a pair of golden eagles appeared on the horizon, tiny specks at first, but growing larger by the second, silently cruising along the spine of the range straight toward me. At the last possible instant the eagles dipped their wings to make a tight circle around the peak, not more than 20 feet from me. An eagle in flight is a huge bird, almost the size of a man, and it looks even bigger; I felt as if I could leap out into space and climb on one of the great muscular backs. Their feathers were burnished gold, smoldering in the low sun. One of the eagles opened its bill to reveal a bright pink tongue, but the birds never made a sound. They circled the summit a second time and departed, rising up into the dark sky in spirals until they disappeared.

According to Konrad Lorenz, eagles are actually rather dim-witted compared to an intelligent bird like a crow, but I suspect eagles are as smart as they need to be, in ways that really matter, well able to survive up to fifty years in the wild. Of course, an eagle's lack of intellect means little to an eagle watcher. Half-baked notions of nobility and wildness aside, eagles obviously have something that human beings do not, and it causes admiration, even envy. There is a strong vicarious element to watching eagles (and to any sort of amateur wildlife study), as if some of the eagle's grace might rub off on the observer if he just concentrates hard enough. Some people become obsessed with it. They become eagle groupies, like my friend in the blue parka, who drives out to Quabbin three or four days a week all season long. He was a short man with a round face, a snub nose, and full cheeks, reminding me a little of something an eagle might prey on, like a groundhog. After we had been talking for a while, he reached into the glove compartment of his car and brought out a 5-by-7-inch color photograph in a gold dime-store frame. It was a closeup of a bald eagle sitting in a tree. The bird looked kind of befuddled, as though it had just awakened from deep sleep.

"I took this last winter with a four-hundred-millimeter lens," the man said. "I was standing right over there. Nobody else was around."

About an hour later the eagles themselves made an appearance, way off on the far side of Quabbin, soaring in the clouds. I could just make them out with my naked eye. Looking through the spotting scope I could see their white heads and bright yellow beaks. They never came any closer.

I never returned to Quabbin, but now, out on the Connecticut River in January, the eagles had come to me. While I was dragging the canoe over the gravel bars I looked up and there they were, three adult eagles and two immature birds, diving and swooping in the air currents, sailing off into the distance and then wheeling around to come back. Agitated ducks, their wings working like eggbeaters as they streaked across the sky, only served to make the eagles look that much more serene, that much bigger. Occasionally an eagle will take a duck, usually when the duck is sitting on the water, but fish make up the largest part of the bald eagle's diet, at least in the summer. During the Atlantic salmon runs, eagles must have flocked to the Connecticut to work the rapids, much as I have seen them do during the steelhead run on the Skagit River in western Washington, where as many as twenty-five or thirty eagles would gather along a single quarter-mile stretch of shallow water, walking along the gravel bars in the rain, ignoring the squalling gulls and the ravens and the fly fishermen, gorging themselves until they could not tear off another chunk of flesh.

I continued upstream. The wind had died some, but there was still the current to contend with, and it began to pick up as I approached a slight drop in the riverbed. All streams, including large ones like the Connecticut, that flow across seemingly level floodplains actually consist of a series of pools and riffles — flat stretches of water interrupted by minor, often barely perceptible drops. The riffles are most noticeable when a river is low, and they occur at fairly regular intervals, usually five to seven times the width of the channel. According to Leopold and Langbein, the steepest parts of successive riffle drops are found on alternate sides of the river, so even when the river is flowing straight, as the Connecticut was now, the current takes a slightly meandering course. A competent poler could have negotiated this stretch without any trouble, but I let the motor do the work, and it looked as though it was going to take some time. The racing current had cut my speed in half.

My feet had gone numb inside the rubber boots; I wanted to walk. With the fastest part of the current behind me, I headed over to the east side of the river, put the canoe behind a fallen tree, and scrambled up the bank, curious about what I might find up there. (The high banks along this reach of river make it hard to see much of anything from the water.) I broke through a tangle of prickers to the edge of a rolling tobacco field planted in some sort of grassy cover crop that was surprisingly green for January. Brown, creosoted tobacco barns marched down the middle of the field in single file, one after the other. There was a white frame house in the distance with a car parked in the dooryard. The hood was up and I could see a figure bending over the engine. Big white cumulus clouds cast shadows in the fields; it was very quiet. I stood still and listened hard: the ubiquitous traffic roar, and all the other usual background noises, were missing. With the motor going before, I hadn't noticed. Wooded hills rose up beyond the barns, off to the east, and there was another range of hills — the Pocumtuck Range, named after an Indian tribe — on the west side of the river. The Pocumtuck Range is actually a narrow ridge; it begins abruptly at North Sugarloaf and runs up along the Connecticut to the mouth of the tributary Deerfield River. The main part of the Connecticut Valley, with the interstate, U.S. 5, and the railroad, is on the other side of the ridge, walled off from the river. That explained the quiet.

By the time I got back in the canoe it was a few minutes shy of two o'clock, and the afternoon light was beginning to take on a fine, mellow quality. The air had that superb, absolutely dust-free clarity that only comes in the winter and makes it seem as though you are seeing true colors for the very first time. Even my ugly yellow canoe looked good, shiny and sleek like a waxed banana. The river was a deep blue, darker and denser than the sky by several degrees. Little gusts of wind ruffled the surface of the water in changing patterns and textures. I had not planned exactly how far upstream I would go, but the day was turning out to be so pleasant that I thought I might as well try for the beginning of the Turners Falls Canal. I wasn't sure how far that was, or, for that matter, how far I had already come, but it wasn't important. With the wind and the current, it would be easy to get back to Sunderland, even in the dark.

Before long, however, the sound of diesel locomotives in the East Deerfield freight yards informed me that I *had* come a good ways. Then the bow of the canoe swung around a bend in the river, and a massive deck truss railroad bridge appeared ahead. As if on cue, a switch engine backed onto the bridge and paused. A puff of black smoke rose from the exhaust stack, and the little locomotive shuddered. It moved forward, stopped, and backed up again, shoving cars into the yard, two and three at a time, letting them roll free onto the proper tracks.

Long after the bridge fell astern I could hear the deep, reverberating rumble of boxcars striking each other as they locked couplers, a sound that I've always liked, especially at night in a motel room in some strange town. Everything about trains is a pleasure to me. My interest in railroads reached a peak when I was twelve or thirteen, then tapered off to almost nothing, only to reassert itself in the mid-1970s. It was then that I discovered East Deerfield, the best place to watch trains in New England.

East Deerfield is the hub of the Boston & Maine Railroad, where the east-west main line from Portland, Maine, to Mechanicville, New York, intersects the north-south Connecticut Valley line. A highway bridge across the tracks offers a bird's-eye view of the yard, and it was here that I first met my fellow train watchers, perched along the railing like pigeons, fully equipped with cameras, video recorders, and portable radio scanners. I was taken aback. It's one thing to nurture a passion in private; to see it in others, revealed and intensified, can be embarrassing, but I soon got over it. It is true that a lot of the romance went out of railroading when steam locomotives vanished in the 1950s, but the noise, and the grime, and the essential, humble nobility of large objects in motion — these things remain. The scale is just a little larger than life. The solid heft of a train is utterly unambiguous, intensely satisfying, and the names on the boxcars have a gritty, bulletproof kind of glamour: Union Pacific, Rio Grande, Bangor & Aroostook, Cotton Belt, Santa Fe — names that speak of distance, of deserts and mountains, of the Railroad Earth, as Jack Kerouac called it.

I hadn't been down to East Deerfield in quite a while, the river having claimed my full attention. Now I came to the mouth of the Deerfield. The Turners Falls hydroelectric power canal, which begins just a little farther upstream, is closed to canoes and all other boats, making a long portage necessary. I decided to go up the Deerfield instead.

The Deerfield River rises in southern Vermont. The lower reaches are shallow and quick running, the clear water alive with riffles and tiny rapids, but the current is not formidable; I had no trouble maneuvering with the setting pole.

In 1819 and again in 1826, plans were put forward to open the Deerfield River to commercial navigation with locks and dams. Promoters saw the Deerfield as an important link in a canal route running west from Boston to Albany or Troy, where it would connect with the immensely successful Erie Canal and thus give Boston a share of the lucrative midwestern freight traffic that was rapidly making New York City the commercial hub of the country. This idea sounded grand in a speech, but there were a number of practical problems, most notably the solid bulk of Hoosac Mountain, a Berkshire peak squarely astride the Connecticut River–Hudson River height of land. No amount of locks would get canal boats over this obstacle; it would have to be pierced with a 5-mile tunnel. The Deerfield canal was never built, but the tunnel was, for the Troy & Greenfield Railroad, an ancestor of the B&M. Construction began in 1852 and ended in 1875, after 2 million tons of rock had been removed from the bowels of the mountain. Hoosac was the longest railroad tunnel in the United States until 1926, and it is still the longest east of the Rockies.

As I poled the canoe up to the railroad bridge that crosses the Deerfield River near the west end of the B&M yard, a long freight was preparing to depart to the west. The turbochargers on the four GP40-2 diesels — 12,000 horsepower in all — emitted a shrill whistle. Manufactured by the Electro-Motive Division of General Motors (as were the diesels on board *Texaco Houma*), the GP40-2 is state-of-the-art American locomotive technology, a thick blunt instrument, brutal as a sledgehammer. The exhaust rumble shook the ground, even at idle. Suddenly the train lurched into motion, the slack between the cars running out in a sharp series of crashes, gathering speed as the engineer notched the throttle open to Run-8, getting a good roll on for the hill, the boxcars and covered hoppers rumbling over the bridge, coming endlessly, banging and swaying . . . eighty, ninety, one hundred and twenty cars, 9,000 gross tons, and finally the caboose, with another locomotive coupled on behind it, pushing hard.

I continued up the Deerfield a piece, then turned around to savor the float back down. The wind had died completely and the sky was luminous; a cold night was on the way. The current moved the canoe in silence, urging it into the riffles and letting it drift in the pools. Far off in the west I could hear the thundering roar of the freight train as it followed the Deerfield Valley up into the ancient heart of the Berkshires, struggling against gravity.

6 ❧ TURNERS FALLS

to NORTHFIELD

Riffle and Pool

GIVEN AN UNLIMITED amount of time, running water will reduce a mountain range to a level plain. The erosion of rock and the transportation of sediment require energy as well as time, and rivers receive their energy from the sun. The process begins with evaporation, when individual water molecules acquire energy as they are lifted from the surface of the ocean into the atmosphere. Part of the energy is lost when the water falls on the mountains as rain, but the remainder is not used up until the water runs down a river and returns to sea level, where the cycle begins again. For its part, the river attempts to minimize energy loss at specific locations along its course by removing or wearing down obstructions in the riverbed, and it tries to distribute energy loss as evenly as possible along the entire length of the course by establishing a uniform, gradual gradient.

The longer a river exists, and the more water it has to work with, the closer it comes to realizing these goals. Thus the tributaries almost invariably have steeper and rockier beds than the master stream, while the gradient of the master stream is steepest near its source. The Connecticut River, which rises at an elevation of 2,600 feet, accomplishes two thirds of its vertical descent to sea level during its first 60 miles. The long profile looks something like this:

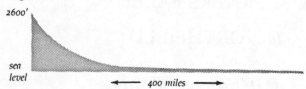

Closer examination shows that a typical 3- or 4-mile section of the riverbed actually has a slightly undulating profile — the standard sequence of riffles and pools. Hydrologic studies have revealed that the slope of the water surface is steeper in a meandering curve than it is in a straight reach, but that the surface slope in a straight reach descends in a series of steps (corresponding to the riffles) while the surface slope in a meander is more nearly uniform. To quote Leopold and Langbein,

> It appears that a meandering channel more closely
> approaches uniformity in the rate of work over the various
> irregularities of the riverbed than a straight channel
> does . . . the meandering form is the most probable result of
> the processes that on the one hand tend to eliminate
> concentrations of energy loss and on the other tend to reduce
> the total energy loss at a minimum rate. The sine-generated
> curvature assumed by meanders achieves these ends more
> satisfactorily than any other shape.

In order for a river to meander, however, it must first create an alluvial floodplain, and the rapidity of this process depends upon the vertical relief and the composition of the landscape. Some rocks are more resistant to erosion than others, with bands of particularly hard bedrock enduring the longest of all, and until these stubborn bands are worn down by the river, they cause waterfalls and rapids. Since the Connecticut River drainage basin is extremely mountainous, with a complex geological history, you would expect to find numerous rapids interrupting the more level stretches of meandering riverbed, and this is the case — at Enfield, Hadley Falls, Bellows Falls, Sumner Falls, and at least a dozen other places.

At Turners Falls, Massachusetts, the rapids were circumvented by a navigation canal for flatboats in 1795. Paper mills were built beside the river during the nineteenth century, and hydroelectric facilities were added later, with a small generating unit at the head of the present power canal and a larger unit at the canal's lower end, near the mouth of the Deerfield River. The paper industry is at least as old as the textile industry, but while textiles have deserted the region, paper is still here in force, employing about a hundred thousand New Englanders. The economy of Maine is dominated by paper, and paper mills dot the banks of the Connecticut River and its tributaries in central Massachusetts. Why the paper industry stayed when textiles headed south is a question for economists to decide, but it must have had something to do with the fact that paper mills, unlike textile mills, never divorced themselves from the rivers. Even where a paper mill doesn't use a river for power (and many paper mills do have their own hydroelectric units), a good supply of running water is essential to the chemical part of the papermaking process. A riverside mill site is usually too valuable to give up.

In Turners Falls, a highway bridge that spans the Connecticut just downstream from the big dam affords an excellent view of the entire complex — the mills, the power canal, and the new fish ladder. The expansive pond behind the dam contrasts sharply with the bone dry, rocky riverbed in the gorge below it, and you can almost feel the immense head of power pressing on the floodgates, straining to be let free. Water plunging down a penstock to spin a turbine is exactly the kind of concentrated energy loss that a river, left to its own devices, tries to avoid. Nevertheless, the rapids at Turners Falls were spectacular in times past, and they still are, for a few days in the spring, when the freshet comes roaring through. Slabby cliffs rise above the west side of the gorge, and it was up there, on top of the cliffs, that George Van Dyke met his end in 1909. Van Dyke was the boss of the Connecticut Valley Lumber Company and the king of the great Connecticut River log drives. River driving was dangerous work, and in his younger days Van Dyke could wield a peavy or balance on a floating log as well as any of his men, but as he grew older he took to following the drive along the banks in an open touring car. The logs tended to jam in the rapids, and it was one of these jams that attracted Van Dyke to the cliff top in Turners Falls. It isn't clear exactly what happened — either Van Dyke ordered his chauffeur to back the car too close to the edge or the chauffeur mistakenly shifted into reverse instead of first — but the car plunged over the brink. The famous timber baron died of multiple injuries a few hours later.

❧

I drove down to Turners Falls to resume my river journey on a gloomy day in January 1983. It had snowed some in the morning; clouds of steam rose from the old brick paper mills and the tires of passing cars hissed on the slick pavement, spraying slush, as I walked out on the bridge to survey the situation. The boat ramps that normally give access to the pond behind the dam were closed for the season, but I managed to find a place in the city park where I could launch the canoe by lowering it down a stone wall. Despite the dirty weather it was not particularly cold, just wet and raw, and I had the feeling that the snow was about finished. I started the motor and headed upstream, cutting a broad, rolling wake on the glassy surface of the pond. Gritty clouds pressed down on the gray hills. A blue strobe light on top of a tall smokestack flashed on and off.

The river above Turners Falls follows a twisting course, and I put up flocks of ducks as I rounded each bend. I could detect no current whatsoever, although there were chunks of ice floating in the water, moving very slowly. Steep hills rose directly from the drowned riverbed, sometimes in overhanging cliffs where massive icicles had accumulated. A gorge or a narrow valley of some sort is usually associated with falls in a river, and this is convenient for dam builders since it provides a basin to hold the pond. A deadwater pond is a poor thing compared to a living river, but not a total loss as far as recreation is concerned. Indeed, the more a river looks and acts like a lake the better many people seem to like it, and there are numerous camps — the New England term for summer cottages — along the shores of the Connecticut above Turners Falls. Most were boarded up for the winter.

The walls of the valley gradually drew closer together as I cruised upstream; then, as the canoe went around a sharp bend to the left, the vaulting steel arch of the French King highway bridge came into view. The Millers River, which appeared to be running in flood, spewing out a fan of silty brown water, emptied into the Connecticut on the right. I turned in at the mouth, but soon encountered a raging current. A shattered crust of white ice extended out into the channel from either shore, and chunks of ice about 10 inches thick and as wide as grand piano lids presented a moving obstacle course as they rolled and bobbed in the turbulent, muddy flow. I hadn't bargained on anything like this. The question was how to extricate myself. Very carefully I let the canoe gather sternway, using the motor as a brake, until I found an eddy where I could turn around and ride the current downstream in the proper manner.

The Millers is a stream that has come back from the dead. Once heavily polluted by paper mill waste and sewage, it has been cleaned up to the point where it now supports trout. The main line of the B&M Railroad follows the valley of the Millers

River up through Athol to Gardner, and the grade there is actually steeper than the one on the climb up the Deerfield Valley to the Hoosac Tunnel. There are stretches on the upper Millers where the riverbed drops 35 feet to the mile, and at one point known as the Funnel it drops 10 feet in the space of 100 yards. The Millers is a worthwhile whitewater run in the spring, as are the Westfield and the Farmington rivers. Given the topography of the Connecticut's drainage basin, any tributary stream with a flow of more than a few hundred cubic feet per second is going to provide good sport for canoes and kayaks. The Chicopee and the Deerfield were once excellent whitewater rivers, but their best rapids have been eliminated by dams.

Back out on the placid Connecticut I continued upstream. By some trick of perspective, the French King gorge does not appear to be nearly so impressive from a canoe as it does when you go out on the high arch bridge and peer over the railing into the depths. With the passage of time, however, the scenery will improve, since falls migrate upriver, deepening their valley in the process. Niagara Falls has moved 7 miles during the past 10,000 years. The excavating power of the rapids at Turners Falls is of course held in check by the dam, but that is just a temporary impediment. The river has all the time in the world.

As I left the French King bridge behind, a large hawk took off from a pine and flew along with the canoe for a while before sailing off. I shut the motor down, swung it up out of the water, and began paddling. The walls of the gorge gradually diminished, giving way to a level floodplain. The river began to go around a gentle meandering bend to the right, and up ahead, on the east bank, I spotted what I assumed was the inlet-outlet of the Northfield pumped storage generating station.

Northfield is a somewhat peculiar installation. Its four great turbines are housed in a cavern-like hall blasted out of solid rock in the center of Northfield Mountain. The turbines run generators capable of producing 1,000 megawatts of electricity — more than most nuclear plants — and the machinery can be brought from a standstill to full speed in three minutes. The reason for putting all this inside a mountain is simple: it allows the water released from the reservoir on top of the peak to fall 850 feet down a pressure shaft before striking the turbine blades. Very few dams are 850 feet high.

The hitch, of course, is that water doesn't get to the mountaintop reservoir by itself: it is pumped uphill from the river. A pumped storage plant is actually like a small version of the hydrologic cycle. The pumps take the place of the sun, raising the water. The water absorbs energy as it is lifted, then releases that energy as it plunges down the smooth-walled pressure shaft — no riffles or rapids here — to run the turbines. But while the power of the sun is unlimited, and free, the pumps run on electricity, and they use a lot of it. For every kilowatt that Northfield generates, 1.35 kilowatts are used during the pumping phase. A pumped storage plant is still economically feasible, at least in theory, because it generates during quiet periods, when surplus nuclear-generated electricity is supposed to be available. In practice, however, coal- and oil-fired plants often provide the electricity that runs the pumps, and Northfield has been accused of actually increasing oil consumption.

If the Metropolitan District Commission (the water utility that serves eastern Massachusetts) has its way, the pumps at Northfield will be given the additional job of removing water from the Connecticut River and sending it through a proposed aqueduct to Quabbin Reservoir. Big as Quabbin is (412 billion gallons — enough to supply all the water needs of the United States, including irrigation and industry, for three and a half days), it has not proved to be big enough to slake the growing thirst of Boston. Northeast Utilities, which owns the Northfield pumped storage plant, is agreeable to the MDC plan, but other people are not. Public opposition, in fact, has kept the project dormant for the past decade.

There is nothing new, of course, about large-scale river diversions, even in nature. The Hudson River, for instance, once drained the Great Lakes, until the St. Lawrence usurped the job. Stream piracy — where one stream cuts through a height of land to capture the waters of an adjoining drainage — is also fairly common. Engineers in Mesopotamia were artificially diverting rivers as early as 5200 B.C., and diverted water is now a way of life in the arid American West. California has one of the most elaborate aqueduct systems in the world. In the humid Northeast, New York City has long obtained part of its drinking water from the Delaware River. In the Soviet Union, a giant diversion project — now on hold — was supposed to take water from three great Siberian rivers, the Ob, the Tobol, and the Irtyrsh, and send it to the desert cotton fields of Uzbekistan. But all river diversions have undesirable side effects, and the plan to pump water from the Connecticut River is no exception. One concern is that fluctuations in the water level, created when the pumps are turned on and off, will lead to riverbank erosion. Another is that a reduced flow below Northfield might allow the tide in Long Island Sound to push salty water farther upstream than it already does. Hydroelectric dams would be affected by the reduced flow as well. A slackened current might also retard the river's natural cleansing processes. Then there is the question of how Connecticut River water would affect Quabbin. At present, the waters of Quabbin are pristine, making up the largest untreated public water supply in the country, but that might change with the introduction of silty river water. Lampreys from the Connecticut River might also find their way into Quabbin, with adverse results for its superb lake trout sport fishery. Finally, there is even some fear that radioactive material from the Vermont Yankee nuclear plant, a dozen miles upstream from the pump intakes, might leak into the Connecticut, enter the aqueduct, and ultimately end up in Boston bathrooms and kitchens. This possibility is remote, but the plant has spilled radioactive water on at least two occasions in the past.

So people are upset. The State of Connecticut took Massachusetts to court back in the 1930s in an unsuccessful attempt to prevent the construction of Quabbin in the first place, and Connecticut opposes the present diversion plan. Citizens of western Massachusetts, traditionally leery of what goes on in Boston, resent the MDC's making yet another grab for Connecticut River water.

In order to deal with the strong emotions and the practical problems created by water diversion, the western states have long since developed a complex body of water law based on prior use and multistate compacts rather than straightforward riparian rights. New England and the rest of the country may well have to come up with something similar because the Quabbin plan, regardless of whether it ever gets past the talking stage, may only be the beginning as far as diversions are concerned. The politics of water, in other words, has come east.

As for the pumped storage plant itself, it is virtually invisible from the river. I put it out of my mind and concentrated on the countryside. The river stretched out in front of me, meandering across its floodplain, much as it had near Sunderland and Hadley. Yet this was not the same valley. It was much narrower, and the tobacco and onion fields had given way to dairy farms. The big cottonwood trees had been absent from the bank for many miles. The Triassic redbeds were nearly gone, too, replaced by older, sterner stuff such as graywackes and schists. In all respects this is a harder country, a colder country. By rights, there should have been a foot or two of snow on the ground. The river should have been frozen. But it wasn't. An hour's worth of steady paddling had forced me to strip down to shirtsleeves.

A flock of ducks flew upriver and set down on the water about a half-mile ahead, raising spray. More ducks, in pairs and threesomes and foursomes, passed high above, disappearing around a downstream bend. I had been seeing ducks all day. There had scarcely been a moment when at least a few ducks had not been in sight. Now they seemed thicker than ever, mostly mergansers, often in big, two-hundred-bird flotillas that made a splashing ruckus when I put them up, rising from the river in clouds, wave after wave of them, until you thought they were all gone; then still more would begin their long takeoff runs, slapping the water with their wings before gaining altitude. The common merganser, a fish eater and a diver, is one of the largest North American ducks, although it is not particularly ducklike in appearance. In fact, it has a slightly raffish look. The bill is thin, with a hooked tip and tiny, sawlike teeth along the inner edges. The female merganser's head is crested, while the male's (which is dark green from November to June, rusty brown like the female's the rest of the year) usually appears to be smooth.

Mergansers are extremely hardy birds, many of them going only as far south in the winter as the first open water. When it's really cold out, when the ice on the river is a foot thick and only the rapids are open, steaming in the subzero air, you can still find mergansers sitting on foam-spattered rocks and paddling around in the eddies, apparently happy as clams. The only time I had ever seen mergansers at all inconvenienced by weather conditions on the river was on a blustery December afternoon up near Windsor, Vermont. The Connecticut was just starting to freeze, and the choppy water was speckled with whitecaps and flat pieces of clear, windowpane ice that raced along on the current, smashing into the canoe. The mergansers were huddled in a mournful group on the shore. I soon gave up myself, but when I turned around to go back downstream I had to meet the full force of the wind-driven waves head on, the canoe pitching and wallowing in the big, smoking rollers. Sheets of spray hit me in the face and chest, instantly freezing to the front of my jacket. In the midst of this I looked up and saw a lone female merganser about 15 feet away (as close as I have ever been to one), bobbing in the rough water like a cork. Sunlight glinted on her brown-crested head, and her red eyes seemed to be laughing.

Today it was almost too warm. I paddled upstream for another hour and then landed on the west side of the river to take a breather, climbing up the bank to a pasture. Although there were still a few miles of Massachusetts left, the wooded hills and the brown cornfields had the look of Vermont or New Hampshire. Off to the east I could see the town of Northfield, the houses standing on the crest of a ridge. In the eighteenth century, Northfield was the last white outpost in the valley, the northern frontier, and was subjected to one Indian raid after another. The Indians are gone now, but this is still hard country. Vermont is still the most rural state in the nation, whereas Massachusetts has long been among the most urban, although perhaps that is too stark a difference. To someone in a canoe, at least, the entire valley seems uncrowded.

For a few moments a bit of weak gold light began to leak through the clouds, forming watery, limpid veins, then it vanished. A loud group of crows came flying by, heading back to their roost; an early January dusk was arriving, and crows do not like to be out at night. They are, quite literally, afraid of the dark. It was time for me to head back, too. As I shoved the canoe into the river, I happened to look down and notice some ripple marks in the bottom mud. I looked again. They were exactly like the fossilized Triassic ripples I had seen near the dinosaur tracks.

7 &. NORTHFIELD
to BELLOWS FALLS

After the Thaw

I LIKE TO STOP by the Riverside Diner in Brattleboro, Vermont, for a late breakfast, lingering with a second cup
of coffee in one of the booths by the large windows that overlook
the Connecticut River. Brattleboro (with a population of 14,000,
the largest city on the river in Vermont) was not built around a
big dam, but it has the look of a mill town, with its frame houses
and compact commercial district. The diner is hard by the riverbank, perched on top of a high stone retaining wall. If the
building stuck out a few feet farther it would be in New Hampshire. The state line is the mean low-water mark on the Connecticut's west shore, so although Vermont and New Hampshire share the Connecticut Valley, they do not share the river
itself. New Hampshire enforces the fish and game laws and is
obliged to maintain the twenty-six public highway bridges between the two states.

Residents of New Hampshire, I might add, do not pay a
state income tax, unlike Vermonters. Nor, on the New Hamp-

shire side of the river, is there a retail sales tax or a bottle deposit. Vermont has both. Vermont has strict land use planning laws; New Hampshire does not. New Hampshire is perceived as pro development while Vermont, if not actually against it, is at least more finicky. The New Hampshire license plate motto is "Live Free or Die"; in Vermont it is "Green Mountains." Yet as you travel up the Connecticut Valley it is difficult to detect any difference in the amount of greenery on the banks of the river. Both sides of the valley are pleasant, neither having succumbed to the supposed ravages of runaway laissez-faire capitalism, despite the repeated attempts at industrial development along the river during the nineteenth and twentieth centuries, in Vermont no less than in New Hampshire. It never really took hold, however, and in all likelihood never will.

What it comes down to is not laws or taxes but the land itself, the stubborn, unyielding, glacier-scraped Yankee landscape. The land is the ultimate arbiter, of course. And of course it is more complicated than that, in the ways that things are always complicated, with qualifications and exceptions, politics and happenstance, but it is the land, always the land, that it comes down to in the end. I sat in my booth at the Riverside Diner and gazed across the water at a steep New Hampshire hillside. Flinty ledges of rock showed through the bare branches of the trees.

The waitress had wandered off to talk to the boys at the counter. At the other end of the restaurant, an old man sat at the bar in front of a Budweiser long-neck, his cigarette glowing in the darkness while a Conway Twitty song played on the jukebox. The river flowed by the windows in the fierce March sunshine, unobserved. My canoe was out in the parking lot on top of the car; I got up and paid the check.

❧

Brattleboro is about 13 miles north of the Massachusetts border. I drove down the valley to the state line and crossed the river to a boat ramp on the east bank near the town of Northfield. A small creek emptying into the Connecticut ran fairly clear, with a glaze of ice on the rocks, but the river itself was brown, turbid, and high, sliding along powerfully through bare, not-yet-thawed fields under a winter blue, absolutely cloudless sky. The momentum for spring was building, but it wasn't quite here yet. The air still had a sharp bite to it; fortunately, there was no wind. The asphalt ramp was coated with slick, silty river mud that clung to my boots in gobs. With a furious burst of energy I set off paddling upstream, lifting the bow out of the water at each stroke in what soon became a hopeless attempt to make headway. I switched to the motor.

About a mile later the river entered New Hampshire, although it would take a cartographer to say exactly where. If I had gone ashore, I could probably have found the monument — on the Vermont side. To end the continual bickering over the precise location of the boundary between Vermont and New Hampshire — which shifts as the meandering river changes course — in 1936 the Supreme Court of the United States had some ninety markers placed at various points along the Connecticut River. You have to hunt for them. I went around a bend and the first landmark that I definitely knew to be in New Hampshire, an abandoned deck girder railroad bridge, appeared ahead.

One of the bridge's tall concrete piers, knocked out of alignment by an ice jam, leaned over at a sickening angle. The entire span looked as if it was ready to go. Granite piers were standard on railroad bridges until the 1920s, when concrete took over. It was cheaper, of course, to pour concrete than to hire skilled stonemasons, but the old granite blocks are unmatched for durability, and bridge builders have begun to use them again, at least on the lower portions of new piers, particularly on the upstream side, where wear and tear are most severe. The recently completed I-391 bridge in Holyoke is an example.

High as the river was this morning, it had apparently dropped some in the last few days because there was flotsam, including a child's red plastic sled, caught in the branches and brush that hung over the water a good 2 or 3 feet above my head. Newly arrived black ducks, mallards, and wood ducks were sheltering in behind downed trees, replacing the winter mergansers that had already flown north. As I approached the mouth of the Ashuelot River, the Connecticut's primary tributary in southeastern New Hampshire, I spotted a swimming muskrat, my first of the season. The wet fur on his back was a rich brown, like an old saddle or an expensive pair of shoes. The Ashuelot was running in flood and I decided to pass it by, having all the fast water I could handle on the Connecticut. Even with the motor running full bore it was making less than 2 miles an hour, and the current seemed to be picking up, just as it should in the last mile or two below a dam — Vernon Dam, in this case.

The Vernon rapids hindered flatboats but did not amount to an impassable barrier, so a navigation canal was not built here. Nevertheless, Vernon became the first dam site in the New England Power Company (NEPCO) hydroelectric system, with construction completed in 1909. The dam is still in use today, and when I finally made my way up to it in the canoe, after much slow going, a substantial amount of water was spilling over the top, indicating that the pond was full and that the generators were probably running at their full 28.5-megawatt capacity. The brick powerhouse, which looks something like the post office in a medium-size city, is on the Vermont side of the river, just downstream from the Vermont Yankee nuclear power plant.

Two basic factors contribute to the amount of electricity that can be generated at a specific dam site: the amount of water flowing in the river, and the vertical distance the water falls (or can be made to fall). In very rough terms, a high dam on a small stream will produce as much power as a low dam on a big stream. The Connecticut River drops 2,600 feet from its source to sea level, but the first 1,330 feet of that drop do not have sufficient flow to be useful for hydroelectric installations, the uppermost river being little more than a brook. About 55 percent (700 feet) of the remaining 1,270 vertical feet has been harnessed by no fewer than eleven hydroelectric dams (plus some storage reservoirs on the uppermost river), spaced over 300 miles, so it is not too farfetched to think of the Connecticut as a series of pools interrupted by sharp drops. This, however, was the basic pattern before any dams were built at all, since the greater part of the course consisted of gentle gradient interrupted by falls and rapids. The dams, of course, were placed at the major natural drops, and all of the best sites have long since been taken. In fact, two former dam sites on the upper river have been abandoned as marginal.

NEPCO supplies power to retail electric companies with customers in Rhode Island, central Massachusetts, and a few towns in New Hampshire. In addition to Vernon, there are five other NEPCO hydroelectric dams on the Connecticut River, with capacities ranging from 13 to 199 megawatts, plus eight hydro dams and a 600-megawatt pumped storage unit on the Deerfield River. All told, NEPCO's fourteen conventional hydro units have a combined capacity of 594 megawatts, about the same as Vermont Yankee, but the figures are not strictly comparable since nuclear plants usually provide base load power, while most hydro plants generate peaking power. Water is stored while the demand for electricity is low, then released to run the turbines as the demand rises. The amount of water that can be stored in this fashion is a third factor determining the potential power at a dam site.

Aside from the NEPCO dams, there are two large Northeast Utilities dams on the lower Connecticut (at Holyoke and Turners Falls) and a tiny Public Service Company of New Hampshire unit way up in Beecher Falls, Vermont, two paper company hydro dams (at Ryegate and Gilman, Vermont) on the upper river, along with numerous dams on the tributaries, mostly in the 1- to 5-megawatt range. Since the peak demand for electricity in New England is between 16,000 and 20,000 megawatts, it is obvious that hydro power from the Connecticut, or from any other river in the region, can supply only a fraction of the total. Of all the electricity generated in the United States, hydroelectric power accounts for 12.8 percent, with coal (46.3 percent), gas (14.8 percent), oil (14.4 percent), and nuclear (11.3 percent) producing most of the rest. There is not much potential for future large-scale hydro development in New England since most of the river valleys are heavily settled and big dams would mean Quabbin-style dislocation. The only practical sites are in northern Maine, and even there hydro projects encounter withering opposition. The proposed Dickey-Lincoln Dam on the wild and free-flowing upper St. John River has been stymied for years, perhaps now for good.

But this does not mean that hydro is dead. Far from it. There are innumerable dam sites on smaller streams — some undeveloped, others with old dams in place, and some with generating equipment that simply needs to be cleaned up a little. Small hydro — or "low head hydro," as it is often called — has a number of things going for it. It doesn't produce acid rain, it doesn't create waste products with half-lives, and — supposedly — it is cheap. Since utilities are obliged to buy electricity produced by private citizens, even the smallest back-yard hydro unit has ready access to the distribution system. There are, however, some disadvantages. The great majority of old dam sites that might seem ripe for rehabilitation are run-of-the-river installations; that is, they are dependent on natural stream flow. Unfortunately, most streams run high for a month or two in the spring and then quickly dwindle off. Generating equipment that can take full advantage of the peak flow is grossly underutilized, or inoperable, when the water drops. The way to get around this is to build a storage reservoir, but it has to be fairly large to be worthwhile. Small hydro, in other words, has a way of getting big in a hurry, at least while a project is on the drawing board, which is where many of them stay. The town of Springfield, Vermont, for example, subjected its citizens to eight years of circular, acrimonious debate and spent $3.1 million on studies, reports, and legal fees before plans for an ambitious municipal hydro system were finally dropped in 1983. Other plans have met similar fates.

ᴄᴡ

The deadwater pond behind Vernon Dam covers 2,250 acres, and I have never felt any desire to take the canoe out on it; you have to go up to Brattleboro before the Connecticut starts to look and act like a living river again. About 3 miles above downtown Brattleboro, a major tributary that the Indians called the Wantasigeset River empties into the Connecticut on the Vermont side. The Wantasigeset (or the West River, as the white men renamed it) rises in the heart of the southern Green Mountains and flows through a steep, deeply carved V-shaped valley along a course full of rocks and rapids. It was a stream that time seemed to pass by, perhaps because of the extreme ruggedness of the terrain. A little railroad was built along the river, but it was abandoned in the 1930s, and the towns of the West River valley stayed small. The Wantasigeset remained a whitewater canoeist's dream. Then, in the 1950s and 1960s, the Army Corps of Engineers arrived with bulldozers and dynamite, putting up not one but two gigantic flood control dams.

Yet this did not totally eliminate whitewater sport on the West River and in one way actually enhanced it. The water level in the catch basins behind the dams is normally kept well below the basins' capacities — otherwise there would be no flood control — but what water does accumulate can be released on demand, in a dribble or a gush, and this is ideal for whitewater competitive events since it eliminates the vagaries of natural runoff. Planners can set the date of a race months in advance, knowing there will be exactly the right amount of water flowing down the course.

I went to watch one of these races, at the Ball Mountain Dam near Jamaica, Vermont, and I was surprised at the size of the crowd. The parking lot, in a cow pasture, was full of cars (heavy on Saabs and Volvos) from twenty-four states. Dozens of tents were set up under the tall pines, and the smoke of cooking fires rose into the air. It was like a tribal encampment, a rite of spring perhaps, with the strongest and the most daring gathered to prove themselves, to pay homage to the river gods — and to compete for places on the United States national team. The needlenose kayaks looked impossibly fragile, light enough to be carried comfortably under one arm, the thin fiberglass hull balanced on a hip. You do not sit down in such a boat; you slither into it as into a tight pair of jeans, then tie a spray cover around your waist.

Huge granite boulders studded the roaring riverbed, dividing the foaming current, raising wild, snowy white waves, and digging deep souse holes. Unlike a normal freshet, the water was crystal clear, all the silt having settled out behind the dam. Simply making it down these rapids alive would have been accomplishment enough, and, indeed, rescue teams were stationed on the shore, but the racers seemed to take survival for granted. Occasionally a boat would flip over, then pop right back up again to continue on. They were racing the clock, maneuvering with incredible precision through a forest of slalom gates, crossing from one side of the river to the other, darting between numbered sets of poles suspended from overhead wires. The level of skill on display here was, quite simply, astonishing. I had never dreamed that a boat could be made to do such things under such taxing conditions. It was the aquatic equivalent of Olympic-class gymnastics. Oddly enough, however, whitewater kayaking is not an Olympic sport, whereas flatwater endurance racing is.

৯৯

Like the canoe, the kayak is an ingenious craft with a distinguished heritage reaching far back into North American prehistory. The kayak does not, however, have the canoe's great versatility or cargo capacity. Among the Eskimos, kayaks were used less as transportation than as hunting aids, primarily to get a man within harpoon-throwing distance of a seal or some other swimming animal. Thus the kayak was a saltwater craft, seaworthy by necessity and able to shrug off big waves that would have filled a canoe instantly. These qualities, enhanced by modern materials and fairly radical design changes, have made the kayak a superb whitewater boat and have allowed it to migrate far from its native habitat — to Vermont, for example — just as the canoe also spread across the continent. But while canoes are still used throughout the same north woods where they were invented, kayaks are virtually extinct in the Arctic, and in a somewhat odd turn of events, many Eskimos now use canoes.

For the next stage of my journey up the Connecticut Valley, however, I wanted to travel on foot, from Putney, Vermont, to Westminster Depot. Linda Hay, who was building a passive solar house in the vicinity, gave me a ride in her ancient VW Beetle to the starting point I had selected, a spot called Putney Great Meadows. The odometer rolled over to 56,483 — the second time around — as she let me out on a dirt road by the B&M Railroad. A few patches of dirty snow still lingered in the fields, with pools of meltwater in the low places, and the crisp March air was chilly enough to make a wool jacket feel good. In the distance, three towering blue metal Harvestore silos rose above a cow barn the size and shape of an airplane hanger, and on the other side of the track was another big dairy farm. Both looked to be three-hundred or four-hundred-cow operations, about as large as you find in the valley. I clambered down an embankment to the railroad and started walking at milepost 72 — 72 miles from Springfield, Massachusetts.

This stretch of the B&M used to be double track — one track for northbound trains, the other for southbound — but when hard times caught up with the railroads in the 1960s the southbound track was removed, leaving a smooth surface that now made for easy walking. You could have ridden a bicycle on it. The cornfields soon gave way to woods, but the leafless trees did not keep the sun out. The shiny rails clanked and popped as they warmed, and heat waves rose from the crushed rock ballast. A pair of blue jays flew across the track, chasing each other. Already I was a little too hot; perhaps the jacket was a mistake. The meandering Connecticut River was beginning to come up close, and at milepost 73 I stopped to sit by the water for a while.

Minnows darted back and forth in the shallows. Pine needles, dead grass, sticks, and small pieces of ice drifted by on the quick current. Yet the runoff had not been up to snuff this year. The winter of 1982–1983 was a poor one for snow. In fact, the last three winters had been kind of anemic. It seemed like a long time since those frigid, almost mythical, January mornings when I used to sit on a stool in the Four Aces Diner in West Lebanon, New Hampshire, at six A.M. and listen to the snowplow drivers lie about the weather. "Thirty-four below out to my place," they'd say, as the slush dripped off their boots and collected in brown puddles on the tile floor. Not this year. The freezeup had been late, and the thaw had come early. I had been out in the canoe every month except February.

Not that it was like a day at the beach. Winter never is. Snow or no snow, the drabness and the short days (pitch dark by four-thirty in the afternoon) are never a tonic. I was glad to see the back of it. And there will be blizzards next year, inevitably. There is no escaping the deep freeze. Even on the muggiest dog days in July, the chill breath of the Ice Age still lingers in these hills, and the scars of glaciers recently departed are everywhere upon the New England landscape.

It has not always been so. There have been long periods when the entire world was warm, but the present glacial age began some 55 million years ago with a drawn-out cooling known as the Cenozoic Climate Decline. As the drifting continents migrated north and south, from the equator to the poles, snow began to linger on the ground in high latitudes. About 10 million years ago an ice cap formed in Antarctica, and glaciers appeared in Alaska. About 3 million years ago a continental ice sheet developed in the Northern Hemisphere. It began to expand and contract in complicated cycles of 100,000, 41,000, and 22,000 years that were triggered by small changes in the shape of the earth's orbit and the tilt of its axis.

New England got colder. More snow than usual may or may not have fallen, but it took longer to melt. Unfamiliar northern animals appeared in the woods. Small alpine glaciers began to form among the high peaks of the White Mountains. Meanwhile, the continental ice sheet was drawing closer, at a rate of 3 or 4 feet a year. Rivers of ice poked into low-lying valleys. Then the entire region was buried, including the tops of the tallest peaks. The ice was more than a mile thick.

From the top of a high ridge in the Cumberland Peninsula of Baffin Island, I once looked down upon a vestigal ice cap. It was white and virginal, noticeably domed in the center, and many hundreds of square miles in area. And it was melting. Filthy, rock-strewn glaciers radiated from the periphery to spawn roaring, milky brown rivers. The freshly exposed landscape had a raw, sullen look. Shattered, pulverized rock lay heaped in huge piles. The weather was atrocious. Sudden gales could flatten your tent as you tried to sleep, and a walker faced the dismal choice of slogging through spongy waterlogged tundra or clambering over miles of sharp, ankle-twisting scree. This was exactly the kind of Arctic wasteland that the continental ice sheet left behind in New England when it finally began to retreat — only to begin another southward advance. Four times the ice came down from the North; four times it withdrew. Every speck of living matter was destroyed in the process. The land itself, groaning under the incalculable weight of the ice, was rearranged on a scale that beggars the imagination. Cirques and ravines and notches were carved out of mountain slopes. Great boulders were picked up and scattered about like pebbles. At its southern edge, the ice dumped billions of tons of morainal material, creating Long Island and Cape Cod. Yet the major landscape features endured. The mountain ranges, although changed in appearance, still stood erect. The Connecticut Valley was not obliterated. Indeed, the river was called upon to carry the greatest runoff it would ever know. As the ice melted, every tributary, every little feeder creek, became a raging torrent. During the height of the glaciation, so much water had been locked up in the ice — removed from the hydrologic cycle — that the level of the oceans had fallen more than 300 feet worldwide. Now that water ran back to the sea. The violence of the runoff, however, was retarded somewhat when a great dam of ice, rocks, and glacial debris plugged the valley at the Middletown Narrows, causing a long, narrow lake to back up all the way into Vermont and New Hampshire. Far larger and far more enduring than any dam ever built by man, the Middletown dam lasted several thousand years, but eventually it broke and the lake drained. As the climate moderated, spruces and firs colonized the disappearing tundra. Then pines and hardwoods appeared, and the land came to look as it does today.

∽

Just beyond milepost 73 the river begins a graceful, sine-generated meandering loop. I found a dead deer here once, smelling it before seeing it, the stink rising off the carcass in thick waves that made me stagger backward. Now, as I walked along the railroad, I spotted a bleached vertebra lying on the ground. It was light in my hand, almost weightless. The track ran ruler straight in front of me on a fill across a flat sweep of bottomland enclosed by the loop. A small cattail marsh in a poorly drained area beside the grade had already been claimed by a red-winged blackbird that defended its territory with loud trills and shoulder patch displays. Crows strutted around in the stubble of last year's corn, and a mob of starlings had gathered in a dead elm. Over in the hills of New Hampshire, snow was visible through the trees at the higher elevations. A new-looking Bush Hog disk harrow, left outside all winter, sat beside a metal-roofed shed. It would be another few weeks, perhaps a month, before tractors could work in the soggy fields without digging deep ruts.

The track went back into the woods, crossed a creek on a short, single-arch stone bridge, and sliced through a rock cut that oozed meltwater. Handsome stone bridges are a feature of this line. The finest example is at Bernardston, Massachusetts, across the Falls River. The bridge, with its seven tall granite arches, resembles a Roman aqueduct. Compared to the lines that crossed the mountains, however, the railroad builders had easy going in the Connecticut Valley. Given the rumpled topography of New England, river valleys invariably offered the best natural rights of way, both in ease of construction and in gentle gradient. Yet the Connecticut Valley never did acquire a railroad that seemed commensurate with the river's stature as the major waterway of New England, and this puzzled me for a while until I saw the obvious answer. The valley runs the wrong way, north-south instead of east-west. A certain amount of freight, mostly paper products, rolls down the valley from Canada, and there is still one Montréal–New York City passenger train left on the line, but the east-west routes, such as the Conrail line through Springfield and the B&M through Hoosac Tunnel, are the primary freight arteries linking Boston to the industrial and agricultural heartland of the Midwest. So too with highways: the east-west Mass. Pike throbs with traffic, whereas I-91, which follows the Connecticut Valley, is often as quiet up here in Vermont as the railroad track I was walking beside.

Well, perhaps not that quiet. I had not seen a train all day and did not expect one until late afternoon. Most of the trains come through at night, which is probably why the deer was killed back at milepost 73. Engineers tell me they turn off the headlight when they see an animal, but many are struck anyhow. I once spotted the hind end of a black bear disappearing into the woods after it ran across the right of way. Another time I met a red fox that was walking toward me along the railhead, apparently mesmerized by his reflection in the gleaming steel. I stood stock still and he didn't look up until he was 20 feet away. He was one very surprised fox.

I was a little surprised myself to see milepost 76 coming up. The walk was going much faster than I had expected. Linda had said she would meet me at five o'clock, so if I didn't slow down I would have a long wait on my hands. But the walking was so easy, so pleasant, that it was hard to keep from striding right along. These mileposts, like the bridges, are granite, quarried slabs with a square cross section 12 inches on a side. The posts stand about 4 feet tall and are sunk an equal distance into the ground. Most railroads simply nail a painted mile board to the nearest telephone pole.

Off to the left, a dairy barn stood next to a house with laundry on the line. Silage that had been chopped last fall and heaped in a pile inside a concrete-walled pit — a "bunker silo" — was about finished now. Holstein cows nosed at hay set out in a feed rack. The village of Westminster, Vermont, was nearby but out of sight, up on a flat terrace rising from the valley floor. Terraces like this, and there are many in the valley, are made of sediment deposited along the edges of the now-vanished glacial lake. The lake's old shoreline, complete with beaches, is supposed to be visible in places. The layers of sediment are called varves, and geologists can trace them year by year, like rings on a stump. They can even tell if it was a wet year or dry year.

A little beyond milepost 78, three dozen cows with yellow plastic number tags in their ears were crowded next to a fence by the track, rolling their eyes at me. They had churned the thawing ground into a black quagmire of manure, puddles, and soupy mud, and their legs and bellies were caked with dried mud. Like all the other cows I had seen today, these were young heifers — the equivalent of teenagers coming to terms with puberty — and they still had a little of the friskiness and the cuteness that would soon give way to solemn bulk. The track began to curve and then a view opened up across the river to Walpole, New Hampshire, up on another glacial lake terrace. A golden weathervane on a church steeple caught the sun. I had some time to kill . . . why not here? I rolled my jacket up to make a pillow and lay down in the warm grass by the river. The current slid by, smooth and powerful. It was not silent; it hissed. Even with my eyes closed I could sense the moving water.

The current gave the flatboats of the nineteenth century considerable difficulty. Most were rigged with a central mast and one or more square sails, but when the wind died the captain relied on a "white ash breeze," provided by the crew and their setting poles. The technique of poling a flatboat was different from that of poling a canoe. You planted one end of the pole against the riverbed and the other against your shoulder. Then you walked the length of the deck — as long as 60 feet — from bow to stern, pushing the boat as you went. After a few weeks of this (and an upstream trip often took a month), a wad of callus formed on a poler's shoulder and the pole fit into it like a peg into a socket. It was not easy work, but then, nothing was particularly easy in those days. The riverboatmen, at least, got to travel. They also smoothed their aches and pains with rum.

It was brought on board by the barrel and consumed at breakfast and supper. A morning libation was standard practice in the valley, ashore as well as afloat. Whole families, including the small children, would line up in the kitchen for a toddy.

I drifted off to sleep. When I awoke, it was a little chilly and shadows were creeping down the bank. The rails had begun to clank again, cooling off now. I almost thought I could hear a train coming, but when I concentrated the sound faded away. Then I thought I could hear it again. I stood up, brushed the grass off my shirt, and climbed back up to the track. A train *was* coming. I stepped off to the side as the headlight swung around the curve, and a single locomotive pulling eleven cars rambled by. It was the little wayfreight that goes up to Bellows Falls from East Deerfield. The caboose bounced and swayed as it diminished down a long, 2-mile straightaway, finally disappearing around a curve by Westminster Depot. A woman stepped out from behind some bushes by the track and started walking toward me with a Saint Bernard on a leash. Her plump, pinkish face reminded me a little of a Saint Bernard's, kind of droopy, but without the sad eyes. Suddenly another train was bearing down on us, coming fast, flushing birds and making cows run. I counted eighty-seven cars — grain hoppers, bulkhead flats, boxes, empty autoracks, superlong LNG tankers that looked like shiny black hot dogs — the great, frantic weight of the thing sending tremors through the ground as the rails flexed beneath the bright, banging press of the wheels. Dry leaves and bits of paper fluttered in the train's wake, gradually coming to rest on the track. I kept on walking. The late afternoon light was nice on the stubble fields, and about a half-mile away cars and pick-ups moved in bunches along U.S. 5. People were coming home from work. Linda pulled into the muddy lot by the old depot a few minutes early, and we drove off toward Bellows Falls.

8 ❧ SOUTHEASTERN VERMONT
and SOUTHWESTERN
NEW HAMPSHIRE
Bedrock

THE LAYOUT AT Bellows Falls, 7 miles north of Westminster Depot, is much like that at Hadley Falls or Turners Falls — a big dam with dry rapids below it, a power canal, old paper mills, and a hydroelectric installation — but Bellows Falls is much more compact, the town being shoehorned into a tight stretch of valley. The B&M Railroad is forced to pass under the main square in a tunnel. There has been a dam of one sort or another at Bellows Falls since 1792, and the present NEPCO hydro facility went on-line in 1927. It has been generating electricity ever since at an average rate of about 228,400,000 kilowatt-hours per year.

For water power you need gradient, and for gradient you need mountains. Vermont has a good supply. The backbone range of the Green Mountains runs the length of the state, from the Canadian border down into Massachusetts, where it is called the Berkshire Hills. Rain falling to the east of the Green Mountains drains into the Connecticut River; rain falling to the west drains into either the Hudson or the St. Lawrence. It is appropriate to think of this terrain in terms of water running downhill since it is running water that has played such a large part in giving the land its present appearance.

In fact, it could be said that rivers are the active component of a landscape, mountains the passive. Mountains don't do anything; they just sit there and get smaller as water wears them down. On the other hand, it is the vertical relief of the mountains that puts the shove in a river's current. The point is worth repeating: without mountains there would be no rivers, and the history of every river is intimately connected to the histories of the mountains within its drainage basin. Running water must flow downhill; it has no choice but to react to the given landscape.

The present Green Mountains are the waterworn stubs of their former selves, dead lumps of ancient stone, but still big enough, and potent enough, to cause considerable inconvenience in the affairs of men. They are cherished nevertheless, or at least rationalized, such is the grace and dignity of these ranges, where every view includes a steeply rising hillside. The mountains, their solidity and their age, are almost a moral force, a key to the Yankee soul. "Flatlander" is the ultimate term of derision.

The original uplift of the Green Mountains dates well back into pre-Panagean times, perhaps 570 million years ago, when the proto Atlantic Ocean was beginning to close. About 500 to 450 million years ago, Eurasia snuggled up against northern North America, lifting the Green Mountains and the northern Appalachians. This event is called the Taconic orogeny,* and it was followed by additional uplift during the Acadian orogeny (about 400 to 350 million years ago) as the plates con-

---

*Mountain-building period; *oro* is the Greek word for "mountain."

tinued to press against each other and shift positions. About 300 million years ago, the southern Appalachians rose up during the Alleghenian orogeny, as Africa seated itself against North America.

The successive orogenies associated with the assembly of Panagea raised mountains in New Hampshire as well as Vermont, but the uplift of the main body of the White Mountains came later, about 180 to 135 million years ago, as the slowly moving North American plate passed over a hot spot in the underlying mantle, and great gobs of molten rock — plutons — began to rise to the surface, creating a mass of towering peaks. They have since been worn down considerably, but even now Mount Washington, where hurricane-force winds blast the summit a hundred days a year, retains an impressive bulk if not the sheer grandeur of much younger ranges such as the Rockies (75 to 40 million years old) or the still-rising Himalayas (25 million years old).

The White Mountains form the northeastern limits of the Connecticut River watershed, separating it from the St. Lawrence, Androscoggin, Saco, and Merrimack river drainage systems. Thus it is convenient to think of the Connecticut as flowing in a crease between the White Mountains to the east and the Green Mountains to the west, although the symmetry is not perfect since a few outlying peaks of the Whites actually extend west of the Connecticut into the northeastern corner of Vermont. In the southern part of New Hampshire, the White Mountains dwindle off into ranges of rolling hills, much like those in Massachusetts. Near the headwaters of the Ashuelot River, however, a bold peak that is obviously made of more resistant rock rears well above its neighbors. This is Mount Monadnock. Its appearance is so striking that the word *monadnock* ("lookout place" in the Algonquin language) has become the generic term for all such mountains.

There are a number of monadnocks in the Connecticut watershed, Mount Ascutney among them. It rises from the Vermont bank of the river near the town of Windsor, and the peak is an unmistakable landmark in the valley, visible to motorists on I-91 as far south as Brattleboro and as far north as Fairlee. A canoeist on the Connecticut is treated to views of Ascutney at dozens of points, all the way from Bellows Falls to White River Junction. At sunset, the triangular profile of the mountain sticks up like a shark fin in a tropical sea. On a clear winter evening, Ascutney's 400-billion-ton mass is a black hole, darker and denser than the blackest night sky. Although Ascutney does not rise from a plain, like a volcano, it is a classic monadnock, not connected by ridges or saddles to any other peaks. You can ride all the way around the mountain on a bicycle without ever gaining or losing more than 500 feet of elevation.

Ascutney is an easy climb, taking no more than a couple of hours from base to summit. Since my house is just a few miles from the mountain's southern flanks I have been to the top many times. Most recently, I took a trail, one of three on the mountain, which began at the end of a dirt road and followed a loud brook for the first part of the ascent up through stands of paper birch and into a beech wood. The forest floor was damp, and the trail itself was running water where the path intersected the dozens of tiny feeder streams emptying into the brook, which rapidly became smaller as I plodded uphill. Soon there were patches of snow in the shade. Then the hardwoods thinned out, and I entered a dense spruce forest where snow covered most of the ground. As I climbed higher, the spruces got shorter and the snow deeper — 3 or 4 feet deep, with a firm, granular crust that was wet to the touch. Mount Ascutney is not tall enough to have a treeline, the mountain being forested to its highest point (3,100 feet), but an old fire tower on the summit provides an unobstructed view over the trees. A few years ago it was possible to go all the way to the top of the tower. Since then, however, the uppermost stairs have been removed. I climbed the two flights that are left and sat down to eat an orange.

Ascutney's massive ridges fell away beneath me, rounded and thick like a fat person's knees, the snow visible through the dark spruces the way pale skin might shine through a leotard. A raven croaked several times, and then I spotted the actual bird, soaring on coal black wings. Far below, the Connecticut ran brown with spring runoff. To the southeast, the Sugar River emptied into the Connecticut on the New Hampshire side, with the old mill town of Claremont a few miles in from the confluence and Mount Sunapee off in the distance, near the Sugar's headwaters. Croydon Mountain — a sharp bump on a long ridge — was much closer, almost directly across the Connecticut from Ascutney. To the northeast, big old Mount Moosilauke, the fifteenth highest peak in the White Mountains, stood out plainly, as did the snowy summits of the Presidential Range, a good 75 miles away. Mount Mansfield and Camel's Hump were barely visible in northern Vermont, but Killington Peak, the second highest in the Green Mountains, bulked large on the skyline a little north of west. Okemo Mountain rose in a rounded lump near the headwaters of the Black River, with Stratton and Bromley to the southwest. Way off to the far southeast the hazy gray profile of Mount Monadnock made a bump on the level horizon.

For every peak I could name there were scores I could not. From the top of Ascutney the face of the earth appeared to be everywhere crumpled, like a piece of foil someone had wadded up into a ball before trying to smooth it out unsuccessfully. Or perhaps a better image would be the violent deformation of sheet metal that occurs when two automobiles smash into each other head-on, considering that these mountains are the result of a continental collision. What is left now is the rubble: smoothed by water and time, ground down by ice, beautiful but not worth very much. A little gold has been found here — Calvin Coolidge mentions it in his autobiography — and some copper, too, as well as larger amounts of talc, marble, and high-grade granite. The ski trails I could see on the sides of half a dozen peaks suggested another sort of wealth. By and large, however, the pickings have been pretty thin.

It has often been said that if the white men had settled North America from west to east that northern New England would still be a wilderness. Perhaps so, but the New England mountains did not discourage the pioneers who came up the Connecticut Valley in the decades after the end of the French and Indian Wars. The hill country rather than the river bottoms was settled first, the hillsides being easier to clear and generally more attractive than the poorly drained swampy areas. A sloping field was not a big disadvantage in an era of small-scale agriculture that made little use of mechanical tools, and although the sidehill topsoil was thin and rocky, it had not been disturbed for a long time and produced excellent crops at first. Its fertility soon began to diminish, however, and erosion increased as the settlers hacked away at the virgin forest. Mill streams ran dry in the summer, and there were flash floods in the spring and fall, with major flooding in 1801, 1811, 1818, and 1826. As if this wasn't hardship enough, there were several epidemics of spotted fever, and a freakish series of summer blizzards in 1816.

Yet all these problems were overshadowed by the fact that the age of subsistence farming was coming to an end. The little hill farm that had supported a man and his family, sometimes just barely, could not produce an adequate cash income. The best solution was often to pack up and leave. It was Horace Greeley, a native of Vermont, who offered the famous advice to head west, and thousands of Yankee hill farmers did just that, especially after the Erie Canal and then the railroads opened up the fertile lands of the Ohio Valley and beyond. It amounted to a mass exodus. By 1890, some 42 percent of the people born in Vermont lived somewhere else. Many of them homesteaded the prairies — John Deere, who invented the plow that tamed the plains, was a former Vermonter; still others went to the cities.

Some became the presidents of great railroads such as the Northern Pacific and the Baltimore & Ohio, and an astonishing number of transplanted Vermonters went into education and politics. All told, Vermont produced 33 U.S. senators, 114 congressmen, 60 governors, and 70 college presidents who served in other states.

There was one cash crop, however, that seemed to be well suited to the New England mountains, and that was wool. Sheep have always been able to get along in hard country, and the demand for wool was rising as the textile industry expanded during the nineteenth century. In 1809, the diplomat William Jarvis purchased a flock of Merino sheep in Spain and imported them to his farm on the banks of the Connecticut River in Weathersfield Bow, Vermont, just a stone's throw from Mount Ascutney. Merinos were unknown in the United States at the time, but they proved to be a superior breed in all respects, and the northern Connecticut Valley soon became the center of New England sheep raising. Many towns in the valley had 10,000 sheep or more. By 1840, there were 617,000 sheep in New Hampshire, 1,681,000 in Vermont — six sheep for every man, woman, and child in the state.

But the sheep craze was short-lived, in part because protective tariffs were lifted from imported wool, in part because as the railroads expanded, huge sheep ranches in the West became more competitive. By 1870, the number of sheep in Vermont had declined by half, tapering off to almost nothing by 1930. At the same time, the number of dairy cows was increasing, surpassing the dwindling sheep count (297,000) in 1900 and climbing still further before leveling off and then falling. The old joke about Vermont having more cows than people has not been true since the 1950s, but dairying remains the dominant type of agriculture in the state.

Today, however, sheep are making a modest comeback, and not just among hobby farmers. A number of large flocks have reappeared in the Mount Ascutney area, one of them belonging to Peter Dunning, a distant neighbor of mine in Springfield, Vermont. When I visited him in the spring of 1983 he was butchering a ewe on the front porch, hacking away at the ribs with a saw. Peter, in his late thirties, seems like a bigger man than he actually is, perhaps because of the force of his personality, which caused him endless trouble in the Marine Corps. Now a full beard and hair combed straight back from his forehead give him the look of a Mennonite elder, and he laughs a lot and keeps big wooden barrels of hard cider down in the cellar. As we stood on the porch, I watched sheep up on a hillside. There were chickens running loose, geese in a pen, hogs snorting in a shed, and a large, charcoal gray rabbit in a cage. A new Holland manure spreader was parked in the dooryard, with elderly tractors standing out in the fields. Sheepdogs barked. Cows bellowed in the barn. Lambs bleated.

Wool from Argentina has made inroads in the United States, Peter told me, and wool from the West accounts for most of the remainder. "There's a wool glut," he said, adding that wool is the minor part of his business. "But I don't want to give you the idea I'd throw it away," he said. "It pays the grain bill."

The way Peter sees it, lamb and mutton have the most potential. He estimates that 70 percent of the lamb consumed in this country is sold in the Northeast and that at the present time much of it comes from New Zealand. There is a market to be exploited, but Vermont growers are not yet numerous enough, or well organized enough, to take advantage of it. Peter sells his lambs on an individual basis, in conjunction with a nearby slaughterhouse.

There are pure-bred registered sheep, of course, just as there are registered dairy cows. Peter has Clun Forest sheep, an English breed introduced to the United States in 1970, and the sale of breeding stock is an additional source of income. "Clun Forest is a good mothering breed," Peter said. "They don't need much help lambing." Hay is the main sheep feed in the winter. "That's the beauty of sheep," he told me. "They don't need much grain, and you can grow good hay here. Sheep make a lot of sense in Vermont." With federal milk price supports under attack, the Vermont dairy industry is increasingly vulnerable, and some farmers have turned to sheep as a hedge against falling profits. "Five years ago dairy farmers laughed at us," Joan Dunning, Peter's wife, said. "Now they come around to ask questions."

∾

If you climb up through the pastures in back of the Dunnings' farm there is a splendid view of Mount Ascutney. When the leaves are off the trees, I can see the top of Ascutney from a second-story window of my own house, but I have never been able to pick out the house from the summit. Almost the entire town of Springfield is hidden in the steep V valley of the Black River, and the valley itself is partially concealed behind hills and ridges. It is not even easy to see the Connecticut Valley from the top of Ascutney except right where the river flows by the base of the mountain. As you look off into the distance, either north or south, the great valley is just one more wrinkle in an infinitely wrinkled landscape. Common sense tells you there is a logic to the drainage patterns, but the eye had difficulty detecting it.

Yet the logic is there, just as surely as it is water running downhill in the river and its myriad tributaries that has shaped the rough work of plate tectonics into its present form. Glacial ice played a role, too, a large role, but the Ice Age was a brief episode in the 450-million-year lifespan of these mountains. A far greater amount of work has been done by water.

Water is the great sculptor, its art that of removal. Even a single raindrop striking a rock will make a mark, however minute. Water grinds, gouges, abrades, smooths, and polishes.

Sometimes it acts with great force, sometimes with a subtle touch, but always with incredible patience and perseverance, and it is ideally suited for its job as chief erosive agent. Water comes close to being a universal solvent. It has a high surface tension. It can carry heavy loads of suspended particles. It adheres to most surfaces. It is extremely stable, and it expands in volume as it freezes. A small amount of water that seeps into a crack can split a huge boulder in two. Water, moreover, has a powerful ally in gravity. Simply doubling the speed of a stream's current increases the weight of the particles the stream can carry by a factor of sixty-four.

Ascutney is a good example of the vast changes that erosion can effect on a landscape. Like the high peaks of the White Mountains, Ascutney came into being about 125 million years ago, when a mass of molten rock rose toward the surface, but the main bulk of the mountain remained buried until erosion removed the material that covered it. The thin air that laps against Ascutney's summit today was once solid ground. If all the material that has been removed from New England since the Green Mountains first rose up could somehow be replaced, it would be at least five times as thick as the greatest ice sheet that ever came down out of the North.

This seems all the more astonishing when you consider that at a given moment, no more than 3 percent of the earth's water supply is circulating through the atmospheric and terrestrial phases of the hydrologic cycle. It is the constant motion, not the sheer quantity of water, that does the work of erosion, but a big river like the Connecticut does not account for much erosion itself. It transports vast amounts of sediment and silt to the sea, but for active erosion it depends on its tributaries, which in turn depend on their tributaries and subtributaries, both to gather water from countless sources and to gnaw away at the land. It is the little streams that are erosion's shock troops, and there are thousands upon thousands of them. Most are too tiny to have names. Many flow for just a few months, or a few weeks, during the year. All are exquisitely responsive to every nuance of the hydrologic cycle, turning gray and murky after a rain, running clear as gin in settled weather.

Tracing the little brooks back up into the hills can be difficult unless you like to wade or bushwhack. A web of dirt roads thread the hills, but they usually ignore the drainage patterns of small watercourses, preferring to run along ridgetops or climb straight up the sides of mountains. To add to the problems of navigation, few roads are marked, and the land is heavily forested. It is easy to end up driving in circles.

But this is nice country to get lost in. The extent of former settlement is remarkable, with old stone walls snaking off into the woods every quarter-mile or so. But if the fields have grown up in woodlots, there are still plenty of people in the hill country, living in hundred-year-old farmhouses, house trailers, split-level ranches, and geodesic domes. Some get by on welfare, others on trust funds. Most work in town, driving down to the valley in the morning, coming back at night.

If you manage to follow a hill stream far enough you will almost invariably find a beaver pond. Beavers set up housekeeping on just about any body of water, including big rivers like the Connecticut, but a stream that is just a little too wide for a man to jump across seems to be preferred. If left alone, the beavers will remain in the same general location for many generations, building additional dams and ponds as the food supply in the immediate vicinity is exhausted. I found such a chain of beaver ponds way back up in the New Hampshire hills on a little headwater tributary of Cold River (which empties into the Connecticut near Walpole).

It was not wilderness — there is no wilderness in New England — but the place had been left alone for a long time. I found an abandoned apple orchard, a few of the trees still bearing wormy fruit, and the traces of an old wagon road, but there were no derelict farm implements or barns fallen down or even any cellar holes. After a few minutes I saw a beaver swimming across one of the ponds. Startled, the animal slapped the water with its flat tail and dove, only to surface again and resume cruising in a cautious orbit, slapping and diving from time to time but apparently curious. At length, the beaver climbed out on a log about 30 feet away and began to groom himself (or herself; you cannot tell a beaver's sex from a distance). It was a big animal, 60 pounds or better, a "superblanket," as the trappers sometimes say.

There were five beaver ponds in all. Only one of them, the newest, had an inhabited lodge. The oldest pond was also the largest, with several acres of open water and a cattail marsh at its upper end. The other four ponds were crowded with dead standing trees. On subsequent visits, as the beavers got used to my presence, I was able to watch them repairing and enlarging the dam, felling trees, chewing the bark off logs, and adding sticks to the winter feed pile on the bottom of the pond next to the lodge. During the spring and early summer, young beavers born the winter before, and still no bigger than small muskrats, would venture out and make bumbling attempts to imitate the activities of their parents. Beavers are admirably equipped for an aquatic life, with closable ears and noses, webbed hind feet, goggle-like clear eye coverings, internal genitalia (like seals'), and special flaps inside the mouth that permit underwater gnawing. Their thick fur, which demands constant care, keeps beavers from ever being wet to the skin. The chisel-shaped orange front teeth continue to grow as long as the animal lives. Although beavers eat lily roots and pond weeds, the food of choice is poplar bark. The main function of the pond is to provide security from predators. It creates a defensive moat around the lodge, which is built as a solid mass and then hollowed out from the inside, making it virtually indestructible.

The pond supports much other life besides beavers. Compared to a fast-running brook, it is a blessedly benign environment. In a stream, most of the smaller animals literally have to hang on for dear life, often by cementing themselves to rocks in a permanent or semipermanent fashion, but the quiet, shallow, sun-warmed waters of a beaver pond allow an incredible array of creatures, ranging in size from the microscopic on up, to breed and multiply. The great bulk of pond life is composed of plankton-like organisms whose presence an observer must take largely on faith. More obvious, however, are the whirlygig beetles, the backswimmers, the water boatmen, and the water striders that live on the surface. Dragonflies and damselflies rule the air, feeding on the clouds of mosquitoes. Newts and salamanders come out in the spring by the thousands, crawling around on the bottom or hanging just below the surface, unwary enough to be caught by hand. Frogs appear to be almost as numerous and just as vulnerable, clasping each other in lethargic, apparently joyless copulation that lasts for hours. The amount of procreation of all types in and near the pond is staggering. By late May or early June, the water near the shore is coated with a thick gray scum of discarded insect larval husks, and great jellied masses of eggs hang in the depths, ready to hatch. Birds attracted to the pond include kingfishers, herons, flycatchers, woodpeckers (who like all the dead trees), grackles, blackbirds, phoebes, sparrows, warblers, wood ducks, and mallards. There are usually a number of muskrats, often living in old beaver lodges. Raccoons, minks, and otters also stop by during their hunting rounds. The otter, which swims right up the underwater tunnels to the beaver lodge, is a formidable enemy, easily capable of killing young beavers if not the full-grown adults.

But despite all of the life, despite the ear-splitting chorus of the spring peepers, the infernal buzz of the insects, and the singing of the birds, not to mention the industry of the beavers themselves, the pond was usually quiet, although not in the sense of lacking sound. If nothing else, there was always the gurgle of water running over the dam, but the pond was quiet in the sense of being peaceful, and after a few visits I found that I could sit still for an hour at a time just watching and listening. The pond became a bright forest window on the sky, a mirror of clouds and bird flight, sensitive to the slightest breath of wind, never the same from one day to the next. It was green and murky with life in the summer, like an organic broth, but it could turn steely gray in a thunderstorm. On cold mornings in the fall the pond would steam. I liked the fall best. The water was clear, either deep blue or amber or jet black, depending on the angle of the sun, and the woods were quiet then, truly quiet. The birds had gone south and the little things, in their millions, were buried in the mud. The pond radiated a shimmering, silky peacefulness that swept over you in waves, powerful and profound, spreading outward like the silent V of ripples behind a swimming beaver's head.

November would give way to December and the snows would begin, sooner and deeper up here than down in the valley. By January the ice on the pond would be a foot and a half thick, with 2 or 3 feet of snow on top of that. I would come out on skis and watch vapor rising from the lodge like smoke from a chimney. If you listened carefully you could hear the beavers moving around inside. Then, one spring, loggers came for the white pine, taking it all and leaving behind big stumps oozing sap and muddy skidder ruts. The beavers had vanished, although I wouldn't want to speculate on what drove them off. A beaver can stand a little chain-saw noise and then some. I have seen beavers build lodges and dams on a stream that flowed down the median strip of an interstate highway.

Of course, these beavers up in the hills would have had to abandon their pond eventually in any case, when they had run through all the poplar — which they pretty nearly had. But poplar doesn't take long to grow back, and some future generation of beavers will colonize this spot. In the meantime, I found a brand-new pond about a mile farther upstream, deep in the woods.

9 ⟡ BELLOWS FALLS

to WINDSOR

The Loon and the Otter

THE OLD Arch Bridge across the Connecticut River at Bellows Falls, Vermont, was supposed to come down on a Friday. It didn't, and I can't say I was surprised. Dropping a big steel bridge with explosives is an art; you want everything just right. The bridge didn't come down on Saturday, either, and when I heard it was still standing on Sunday afternoon, I decided to drive over and take a look.

About seven thousand other people had the same idea. They were lined up along Rockingham Street and Canal Street. They were standing on the flat plot of ground by the dam where the old Rutland Railroad roundhouse used to be. They were perched on rooftops across the river in North Walpole, New Hampshire. Light aircraft circled overhead in the gray December sky. The entire police force was on duty to keep order. I studied the crowd. The worn, work-hardened faces were a good match for the gritty brick of the buildings and the dark-timbered hills rising above. Deer season was over, but the younger men still wore their blaze orange hats. Old-timers had come down to the river in wheelchairs. The light was in their eyes now. They were ready for a catharsis of noise and smoke.

Bellows Falls is a classic river town, although, as I mentioned before, the Great Falls here are dry most of the year. You can find some potholes in the gorge that a grown man would have difficulty climbing out of, suggesting the incredible power of the former cataract, and this is confirmed each spring when the dam's twin 200-ton roller gates are opened to pass the freshet, resurrecting the rapids in a thundering torrent. The ground shakes. A soaking, billowing mist hangs in the air. The water is brown and creamy, like a coffee milkshake, a wild, tumbling mass of explosive waves. Every square inch of river surface is churned into seething, angry froth. "Whitewater" does not begin to describe it. The best kayaker that ever lived could not survive this maelstrom (although a daredevil in an inflated rubber suit once came through unharmed). It was beyond the ability of shad to ascend the Great Falls (this was the historic upstream limit of the shad spawning run), but the salmon somehow were able to do it — and will do so once again with the help of a new, 62-pool fish ladder.

Because the gorge is narrow and deep, with steep rock walls and a convenient rock island in the middle, it was a natural place for a bridge, and the first bridge anywhere on the Connecticut was built here in 1795. A canal with ten locks and a vertical rise of 52 feet was completed in 1802, and it carried flatboats and lumber rafts for fifty years. In the meantime, some seventy waterwheels were tapping the power of the falls for mills and factories. The International Paper Company had a large mill here, but it closed after World War I, as did the Vermont Farm Implement Company, the other major employer. Then NEPCO built the present dam and converted the navigation canal to hydroelectric use, funneling water to 50-megawatt generators in a powerhouse at the base of the falls.

In 1904, the Arch Bridge was built a few hundred yards

above the dam and the head of the gorge, and for several months it was the longest span (650 feet) of its kind in the world. It was also a relatively lightweight bridge, which gave it a graceful appearance, but by the early 1970s its condition had deteriorated to the point where the New Hampshire highway department declared it unsafe for automobiles. Pedestrians were barred from the bridge in 1981 and the roadway deck removed in the fall of 1982. Now the great steel arch itself was about to come down.

But when? That's what we all wanted to know. Some of the spectators had been keeping a vigil since Friday morning, their Instamatics at the ready. Finally, late Sunday afternoon, a warning horn sounded three blasts. The explosion a few minutes later was loud, and it produced a satisfactory cloud of evil-looking greenish-yellow smoke, but nothing happened to the bridge. It didn't even shake. A second charge was set off an hour later with the same result. This time the crowd cheered. People turned to each other and said how they'd known all along that the old bridge was stronger than it looked. I gave up and went home.

❧

According to my count, 79 bridges cross the Connecticut River — 58 highway bridges, 20 railroad bridges, and 1 combination railroad-automobile toll bridge — and two ferries. Heaven only knows how many bridges there are on the tributaries. The total probably changes from week to week, but whatever the actual number, it increased by one in August 1982 when a brand-new covered bridge was put into place across Saxtons River, a minor tributary that empties into the Connecticut just below Bellows Falls. The original hundred-year-old span had collapsed when a ten-wheel dump truck loaded with gravel ignored a posted 2-ton weight limit. This kind of accident had happened before in Vermont, and the normal procedure was to shed a few tears over the splintered wreckage and then replace it with a modern span. In this instance, however, a man over in New Hampshire said he could build a new covered bridge for less money than it would cost to build a steel bridge. A wooden bridge won't take as much weight as a steel bridge, but wood has the advantage of being impervious to road salt, steel's arch enemy. Furthermore, a bridge with a roof on it is not subject to snowplow damage. With minimal upkeep, a covered bridge will last a century — two or three times the average life of a small steel bridge.

During the winter of 1981–1982 I drove by several times to watch the bridge taking shape in a snowy pasture beside Saxtons River, and with the latticework of the truss timbers still unsheathed by the roof and walls, the span reminded me of a great wooden ship on the ways. In August the finished bridge began its four-day, 300-yard journey to the water. A yoke of oxen ploding in a circle around a capstan on the far bank provided propulsion, and the bridge in motion had a ponderous, creaking sort of majesty as each revolution brought the 100-ton span a tiny bit closer. First it moved on log rollers, then it crept out over the river on temporary cribbing. Milton Grayton, the silver-haired seventy-three-year-old bridge builder, surveyed the proceedings with remarkable serenity.

I skipped the dedication ceremony but went back a month later to see how the bridge looked in daily use. It looked smaller. And it still looked brand new, the wood still the color of fresh shavings. Apparently it was not going to be painted. Various covered bridge societies had stapled certificates of authenticity to the inside of the bridge, and I couldn't help feeling a little reverent myself. Big timbers always seem to have that effect; I've noticed the same thing inside old barns. A thousand white oak pegs, each one as thick as your wrist, held the truss timbers together. Wooden pegs are better than bolts. They won't rust or grow brittle, and they give the bridge just the right amount of flex. I was delighted.

❧

In Bellows Falls, the Arch Bridge came down on Monday morning, with only a few die-hard spectators on hand. Additional explosive charges had been tried, but the bridge seemed to survive them all. It chose its own moment to go, quivering for a few seconds and falling over sideways. When I drove by that afternoon, a pair of divers were inspecting the submerged wreckage. There was nothing to see from the shore; the entire bridge had disappeared, just like that.

Work on a new bridge started almost immediately when a crane began to unload long steel I-beams from railroad gondola cars. A few other people had drifted over to watch, and I asked the fellow standing next to me if he had any idea of what was going on. He said the beams were to be driven into the ground to make a foundation for the piers and the abutments. The river, he said, was 38 feet deep, with a gravel bottom underneath silt. The remains of the old bridge would be cleared away later.

He neglected to mention that he was the man in charge, although I had begun to suspect as much. I didn't know the first thing about building a bridge. I had helped put up some temporary bridges when I was in the army, but that simply involved assembling prefabricated panels and maneuvering them out over the stream in much the same way that the Saxtons River bridge had been put into place. This was different.

The new bridge will be of the deck girder type. Instead of vaulting across the river in a single great leap, as the Arch Bridge did, it will have two intermediate piers, relying less on clever design than on the strength of the materials. Take a look around sometime; these concrete pier–steel girder bridges are everywhere. Piers are now routine in places that would have defeated most turn-of-the-century bridge builders; deep water and unstable riverbeds are taken in stride. The steel I-beams used as the pier foundations for the new Bellows Falls bridge appeared to be about 50 or 60 feet long and pointed on one end. To prepare the foundation, a beam would be driven straight into the riverbed by a pile driver on a barge, then a second beam would be welded to the top of the first and driven in also. Each pier required thirty-five or forty beams. Next, a watertight cribbing was put on the foundation and concrete was poured. Once the piers and abutments are finished, the only thing left to do is to swing the girders into place and lay the roadway. It's all very simple, very solid, and very time-consuming. The Arch Bridge, despite its thousands of rivets and welds and elaborate superstructure, was completed in four months (during the winter, using the ice to support the scaffolding), whereas the new bridge will take two years.

❧

According to NEPCO, the long, narrow pond behind the Bellows Falls Dam covers 2,850 acres. It looks more like a river than a lake, however, and that's the way most people think of it, although anyone familiar with free-flowing sections of the Connecticut will notice the difference immediately. The water level changes frequently, not with the seasons or with rainfall, but depending on whether the dam is generating electricity or not. The bottom is silted, and the current, of course, is slack. The normal riffle-pool pattern of the flow is obliterated. Canoeists would call the pond deadwater, but that is a slight exaggeration. There is always *some* current, albeit a barely perceptible one, and in the spring, when both of the dam's floodgates are open, there can be a strong current. Most of the time, however, a canoeist will not be able to detect much difference between paddling upstream and paddling downstream. The wind is likely to be more of a hindrance than the current.

But when the wind dies you can enjoy yourself on the pond. Few things in life are more pleasant than a canoe coasting in absolute silence on glassy water. I prefer a pristine north woods lake just after dawn, with plumes of golden mist rising into the air, but the Bellows Falls pond is a satisfactory substitute. On a warm day I like to go out on the pond and read, or lie down in the bottom of the canoe on a mattress of life jackets and simply drift. There is a surprising amount of wildlife on the pond, too, particularly birds, who stop off here in great numbers during migration. There are other creatures as well. In April 1983, for example, I saw an otter. It surfaced right beside the canoe, the splash making me look up from my book. A close, one-on-one encounter with an otter is always memorable, and later, I couldn't help remembering how my friend with the spotting scope down at Quabbin seemed to get a vicarious lift from watching the eagles. This otter evoked a similar response in me. An otter's grace in the water is unsurpassed; he can outswim the fastest trout, turn on a dime, and follow an underwater scent like a bloodhound. And an otter, unlike many predators who have superior physical talents, is smart as a whip. The otter even seems to have a sense of humor. He spends more time playing than he does killing. This otter on the Bellows Falls pond, obviously unafraid, regarded me curiously for a few minutes, then disappeared under the surface with the fluid motion of a snake. I saw him again a little later, climbing out on the bank and going into a hole under a tree root. There was a pile of clamshells next to the hole.

The next day, out on the pond once again, I saw a loon, although I didn't quite believe it at first. Loons nest on some of the northernmost lakes in the Connecticut watershed but are scarce even there. To find one here on the river this far south was unusual, as Joan Dunning agreed when I told her about it two days later. In fact, Joan wanted to go out and see the loon for herself. It wasn't much of an afternoon for canoeing — the sky was full of dark thunderheads, along with some patches of blue — but the loon wouldn't stay around forever. I was thinking it might have already left for the north country, but on the road to the NEPCO boat ramp near the mouth of the Williams River, Joan spotted an osprey sitting in a tree, which seemed like a good omen.

When the Bellows Falls dam was built, the impounded water spread over the bottomland by the mouth of the Williams River, creating an extensive area of shallow setbacks and swampy wetlands. I was poking around out there on a raw, windy day last November, and as I turned around to head back, another canoe — an old aluminum clunker with a back-yard camouflage paint job — slipped out from behind a cattail island. A skinny kid was paddling bow, with a big, long-haired fellow in the stern. They passed me and landed first. The big guy was wearing a baseball hat and muddy hip boots, just as I was, but he had a handgun in a black leather holster on his belt. He stood there on the bank, hands on hips, squinting out over the water.

"I hope you ain't been doing what I think you have," he said. He was a trapper and thought I might be horning in on his territory. I denied it, but he didn't believe me; then I mentioned that I hadn't seen much muskrat sign anyway.

"I was watching you," he said. "You didn't move around like no duck hunter." Then he became reflective. "I've been trapping this setback fifteen years," he said. "It used to be nothing to take two hundred 'rats out of here a week. Now it's shot. It's the spring season that did it. The 'rats don't have a chance to breed. Let up on it awhile and they'd come right back."

In the meantime, his friend had dragged their canoe over to a pickup truck and raised the hood. He was peering in at the engine. I went about my business and then heard the big guy cursing — I assumed because the truck wouldn't start. Tough luck. I drove off a few minutes later and passed the two of them on the road to the highway. It was just about dark, but they didn't seem to be about to ask for a ride. I stopped anyway. The big fellow said he had jumper cables, so I turned around and gave his truck a start off my battery. He didn't say a thing — just stood there and looked disgusted, grunting a little. His sidekick seemed to be embarrassed.

Since then I have run into the two of them several times, and after the trapper convinced himself that I wasn't any competition he got friendlier. Once he showed me a yearling dog fox, one of the most beautiful animals I have ever seen, with fur the color of autumn sunlight and white teeth like little needles. "There's a little too much black on his belly," the trapper said, running his hand through the fur and pulling out a tick. "Other than that, he's perfect." The fox, he said, was worth $60. Muskrats bring $3 to $5 each. An otter is $50. Fishers bring $170.

I told Joan about the trapper as we were putting the canoe into the river. It looked as if it would rain any minute, and the NEPCO picnic area was deserted. The Connecticut was silty, with a fair current, and I used the motor in deference to a headwind. Joan sat in the bow, scanning the water with binoculars. I aimed the canoe toward the New Hampshire side, and after a half-mile of slow going we rounded a point of land where the river makes a bend to the right, through cornfields. There was a tall tree out on the point, and a second osprey sat in the top branches. "Watch how he swivels his head around," Joan said.

Now she was pointing at something up ahead, two dark-colored birds that were large enough to be loons. But the ease with which they lifted off the water ruled that out. A loon needs a long takeoff run, like a float plane. These birds were cormorants. The loon was in the same place I had seen it two days earlier. Now it was diving. It would stay submerged for what seemed like a full minute (but probably wasn't) and come up at some completely unpredictable spot, often 100 yards from where it had disappeared. I thought I saw it swallow a fish, tipping its head back to get it down, but Joan said it was just a piece of weed. She told me that loons return to the same nesting lake year after year and probably take the same mate, although the male and the female migrate separately and winter separately. This particular loon was biding its time, waiting for the ice-out up in the north woods.

Joan and I decided to go on up the river ourselves before the bird was completely spooked. The water was shallow on the Vermont side, with cattails thick along the bank, but there were no muskrat houses, although a few years ago this whole area was swarming with 'rats. I used to see them swimming under the canoe, each animal leaving a faint trail of silver bubbles. The Indian name for muskrat was *musquash*, and old-time Yankees up here call them "mushrats."

Joan told me that one winter she and Peter had skated down the Connecticut from Springfield to Bellows Falls. Peter had put his foot through the ice near the mouth of the Williams River, and the leather part of his skate froze up so hard that he couldn't get it off until they got home, and only then after warming it in front of the stove for the better part of an hour. The ice on the setbacks is perfectly safe — strong enough to support ice fishing shacks — but the river ice does not inspire confidence. It pops and cracks incessantly and loudly, like rifle shots, and sometimes it chirps like a bird. Even in the coldest weather you still find sinister-looking gaps of open water.

But winter was long gone, although even now, in late April, the stubble fields still looked as brown and lifeless as they did when the snow melted. The birds, however, were coming back. A great blue heron flew across the river, its long legs dangling, and a little later when we landed to take a walk, we flushed three more herons out of a swamp. I also heard the excited, chattering call of a kingfisher. The snowgeese had already come up the valley, first passing over Springfield on April 10, as they do every year, and for several days and nights afterward sweeping across the sky in great wavy Vs, brilliant white against the storm clouds, like animated calligraphy.

As Joan and I got back in the canoe, the hills over in New Hampshire dissolved in the blur of a hard rain. We shoved off and headed downstream. Liquid manure had just been spread on the cornfields in chocolate brown swaths, and the stink was powerful, although muted somewhat by the cold. The violent downpour I expected never came, but it did rain some and then it sleeted. A sharp wind raised a chop in the river that splashed Joan as the bow smacked into the waves. Barn swallows flew low over the water, the blue of their backs seeming especially electric in the dim light.

The sleet stopped and the loon was right where we had left it, still diving. In bird-watching guides, the loons come at the front of the book because they are generally considered to be the least advanced, in evolutionary terms, of all North American birds. There is scientific disagreement about this, but the loon may well have existed in something close to its present form for the past 60 million years, almost since the time of the dinosaurs. There is definitely something primitive about loons, something eerie. A loon doesn't quite seem to be of this world. How much of that is in the loon itself and how much comes from the loon mystique I couldn't say, but the bird is spellbinding. The wail of a loon, at night in the north woods, goes straight through you, touching the lonely place in your soul like no other sound on earth. This loon on the river was silent. I would have liked to watch it awhile longer, but it was getting bitter cold — and dark. We paddled back to the car.

❧

On May 3, I continued upriver in the canoe from the place where Joan and I had turned back. Spring had arrived in the interim. Heavy rains had brought the green up in the fields, and the trees were starting to leaf. The hillsides looked as if they had been dusted with pale green chalk powder. The Connecticut was high, with a strong, silty current, and I had to keep a sharp eye out to avoid striking logs; I don't believe I have ever seen so much driftwood — and other junk — in the river. Along with bottles, plastic containers, six-pack rings, and pieces of lumber, I spotted a perfectly good canoe paddle floating in the water and stopped to fish it out. The woods in the setbacks were flooded, and the cut banks along the main river were close to being over-topped in places, with chunks of sod continually breaking off as the soft dirt gave way.

After a spell I passed the NEPCO boat ramp in Charlestown, New Hampshire, not far from the site of Fort Number Four, built in 1743. Charlestown was the northernmost white settlement in the valley at the time, like Deerfield and North-field before it, and the fort acted as a lightning rod for Indian raids. The final French and Indian War began in 1755, and though no major battles were fought in Charlestown (or any-where else in the valley), Fort Number Four had strategic im-portance because of its location at the eastern end of the Crown Point military road, which crossed the Green Mountains from the Connecticut River to Lake Champlain.

It was from Crown Point, then the headquarters of General Amherst, that Major Robert Rogers and his troop of rangers set out on a punitive raid against the St. Francis Indians in 1759. Québec had already fallen, but Rogers didn't know that. He and his men rowed up Lake Champlain in longboats, then traveled overland to the unsuspecting village of St. Francis, near the con-fluence of the St. Francis and the St. Lawrence rivers. Rogers attacked at dawn, slaughtering some two hundred men, women, and children, looting and burning, freeing white cap-tives, and fleeing south toward Lake Memphremagog (on the Vermont-Québec border) under close pursuit. At Memphrema-gog the rangers split into small groups, meeting later to journey down the Connecticut River, first on foot and then by raft, to Fort Number Four.

More than two-hundred years later, when I was a private in basic training at Fort Dix, New Jersey, we were given wallet-size copies of "Rogers Rangers Standing Orders." I have forgot-ten what those orders were (if I ever bothered to read them at all), but I imagine they had something to do with Rogers' con-cept of guerrilla warfare, and the army thought it might con-ceivably apply to Vietnam. Rogers' Rangers, it seems, were the Green Berets of their day, and the Major himself was known among the Indians as Wabo Mahondo, "the White Devil." He believed in Indian-style tactics and was reputed to be a master tracker and woodsman. The son of a poor New Hampshire farmer, Rogers earned fame for his exploits both here and in England, but he never really was accepted by the British military establishment. Oddly enough, however, he sided with England during the Revolution. It was the St. Francis raid that put Rogers in the public eye, and the retreat down the Connecticut River captured a good share of the attention, mainly because it entailed such hardship. Northern New England was an unexplored wilderness in those days, a hazardous place to travel under the best conditions, but Rogers faced the additional danger of sudden attack by the enraged Indians who were pursuing him. Hunger was a more immediate concern, since the rangers were moving too fast to hunt and could not fire their rifles regardless, for fear of attracting attention.

By the time the men reached the Connecticut, they were half dead from starvation. Having anticipated this outcome, Rogers had arranged for a relief party from Fort Number Four to meet the rangers at the confluence of the Connecticut and the Ammonoosuc — the present town of Woodsville, New Hampshire — but the rescue party, after waiting for a few days, had headed back to Charlestown just a half-hour before the rangers straggled out of the woods. Finding the campfire ashes still warm, Rogers fired signal shots in the air, which the commander of the rescue party mistook for an Indian attack, prompting him to turn tail and race down the river. Rogers then built a raft and set out for Fort Number Four with two rangers and a captive Indian boy, but the raft was destroyed in the rapids. Rogers built another raft and pressed on. He finally arrived at the fort, and two days later he headed back upstream with canoes full of supplies for the rest of the men.

Now, in May 1983, a flock of twenty-five white gulls floated peacefully in the middle of the Connecticut. I was approaching the mouth of the Black River, on the left, with the Springfield-Charlestown toll bridge a couple of hundred yards above the confluence. A pair of black-crowned night herons sat in a tree branch hanging over the bank. I presume they were migrating. The toll bridge is owned by the Springfield Terminal Railway, a former trolley line that is now a subsidiary of the Boston & Maine. The turbulent wakes fanning out behind the stone bridge piers revealed the power in the current, which was increasing with every mile I traveled upstream from the Bellows Falls Dam. I shut off the motor and tried paddling for a while, but soon gave up. A man on the Vermont side was mowing his lawn with a little riding mower, and he made five or six passes in the time it took me to paddle the length of his yard.

Back in 1772, just thirteen years after Rogers' raid on St. Francis, things were quiet enough in the valley for a Dartmouth student by the name of John Ledyard to make a purely recreational voyage down the Connecticut, all the way from Hanover, New Hampshire, to Hartford. Dartmouth College had been established in Hanover just two years earlier, in 1770, for the stated purpose of educating the Indians. Unfortunately, there weren't many Indians left to attend classes. If there had been, they would probably have advised Ledyard to use a bark canoe on his trip, but he chose a 50-foot white pine dugout instead. It must have been a handful for one man to paddle, although in those days not much paddling was necessary, for the current did most of the work. There was not a single dam on the Connecticut to retard the flow. In fact, Ledyard was lying in the bottom of his canoe reading Ovid as he drifted down on the rapids at Bellows Falls, but he roused himself in time to scramble ashore. Oxen carried the heavy canoe around the gorge. For his arrival in Hartford, some two weeks later, Ledyard put on a bearskin robe, causing a sensation.

About an hour and a half after I passed under the Springfield-Charlestown toll bridge I came to the mouth of the Little Sugar River, on the New Hampshire side. The woods nearby were partially flooded, and where they weren't actually inundated, the forest floor was bright with new skunk cabbage and fiddlehead fern. The water coming down the Little Sugar ran crystal clear, with a faint golden color that it took on from the sandy bottoms of the deep, quiet holes at the mouth. The tributaries always clear up quicker than the master stream. I leaned over the side of the canoe and saw a pair of monster bass dart away into the shadows. Off to the northwest Mount Ascutney rose in the distance, about a dozen miles away, and as I continued up the meandering Connecticut the mountain seemed to shift position, like a great blue cloud drifting across the sky, appearing to be first on one side of the river and then the other. Presently a commotion erupted in the bushes, and I turned around in time to see a big black beaver sliding headlong down the bank on his belly. A beaver's first instinct upon sensing danger is to get wet as quickly as possible, sometimes with unexpected consequences. This beaver hit the water a safe distance away, but once when I was poling close to the shore a beaver hurtled over the lip of the cut bank in a blind panic, right above my head, and nearly landed in the canoe.

I passed Hubbard Island, and in another mile I came to an extremely sharp bend to the left where the abrupt change in direction made strong whirlpools on the inside of the curve. I stayed close to the outside bank — the New Hampshire side — and surprised a fat groundhog dozing in the sun. He sprinted alongside the canoe for a bit, in that lumpy groundhog gait, before diving into his hole. Seconds later a small dark animal plopped into the water. It could have been a muskrat or even a turtle. Sandpipers were out and about; I had been watching them all day. There seemed to be three or four different species. I passed Jarvis Island, named for the man who brought Merino sheep to Vermont, slowly on the left, and the river curved around to the right, heading north again. The hills on either side began to close in until there was no floodplain left at all. Barber Mountain, on the New Hampshire bank, rises to 961 feet, and there are several points on the Vermont side that top 800 feet. The river itself is about 320 feet above sea level, flowing through exactly the type of narrow, constricted passage where you would expect to find rapids, but there are none.

There is, however, a small Vermont state park nestled in a grove of pines on the west bank where I launched the canoe once. The campground tender and his wife spend their winters in Texas and come up here each summer. It has given them a lot of time to watch the river, and I enjoyed talking to people who took a keen interest in the rise and fall of the water level, the strength of the current, the wind, the siltiness of the water, the bird migrations, and all the other minutiae that have come to fascinate me, to the point of obsession, during the past year. I can't explain it. The river is the river; it's going to work a spell on you, whether you get out on it in a boat or just stay in one spot and let the water flow by your doorstep. Either way, the endless motion is hypnotic, and after a while it becomes addictive. Time is all it takes. The river will get to you before long, and then you are hooked.

Some people want to see the whole thing; others are content to ply the same stretch of river over and over again. The pilot of the tugboat *Texaco Houma,* who took as much interest in the Connecticut as anyone I have met, had never been north of Holyoke. Nor had the rest of *Houma*'s crew. By the same token, there are licensed guides up in the headwaters of northern New Hampshire who have never seen the Connecticut's mouth and apparently feel little urge to make the trip. I can understand that. It is not necessary to see every last mile of riverbank in order to comprehend the river as a whole, at least in a spiritual sense. Indeed, an intimate relationship with one particular stretch of river can be just as rewarding as a survey of the entire watershed, perhaps more so. It depends, I suppose, on your temperament. My own inclination is to get in the canoe and investigate new territory, and with the state park behind me I figured I had now come about halfway from the Sound to the source, give or take a dozen miles.

The river had changed considerably, albeit gradually, in 200 miles. Although still a sizable stream, it is, of course, much narrower up here. Bridges now run about 450 feet long, compared to more than 1,000 feet down in Springfield or Hartford. The average flow here is about 8,500 cubic feet per second compared to 16,470 at Enfield Rapids. But the bulk of the vertical descent from the headwaters, some 2,280 feet of it, still lies ahead.

Yet the gradient, except for occasional rapids, does not steepen significantly for at least another 140 miles. Less than a quarter-mile above the state park canoe landing, the hills that press close to either bank moved back, giving way to a level floodplain once again. The river had spilled into some cornfields on the New Hampshire side; never having canoed in a cornfield before, I took advantage of this opportunity to give it a try. About ten days earlier, before the rains began, trucks were out spreading lime in the fields, and a huge four-wheel-drive articulated tractor was pulling a seven-bottom plow. Much of that work would have to be done over.

The Sugar River, which rises from Lake Sunapee, the largest natural body of water in the Connecticut's drainage basin, empties into the Connecticut nearby. Like the Black, the Deerfield, and the Chicopee, the Sugar River is another one of those tributaries that flows down a virtual staircase of dams, but it also manages to squeeze in one of the pleasantest whitewater runs you could ever hope to find, as Peter Dunning and I discovered later in the summer. Now a large number of swallows skimmed along the smooth water at the Sugar's mouth, just high enough above the surface so their pointed wingtips did not touch it on the downstroke. Whatever sort of insects the birds were chasing were too small for me to see. As fast as the swallows flew, they could make instant changes in course, jerking to the right or left, diving and climbing, suddenly reversing direction. They paid the canoe no more attention than they would have given a floating log.

Mount Ascutney rose up across from the Sugar River, very close and very big now. I continued up the Connecticut, gradually drawing even with Ascutney's summit, then leaving it behind. Windsor, Vermont, was around the next bend, where the river begins to run in riffles, and a few miles beyond Windsor I knew I would find Sumner Falls, but not that day. It was getting dark, and I had to quit, reluctantly.

10 ❧ WINDSOR
to THETFORD

Tributaries

 W HITE RIVER JUNCTION, VERMONT, 14 miles north of Windsor, is the crossroads of the upper Connecticut Valley by virtue of its location at the confluence of the White River and the Connecticut River. The White River is the Connecticut's major tributary in Vermont, and the gentle gradients of the White River valley provided a natural railroad route into the heart of the Green Mountains where the adjoining watershed of the Winooski River gave easy access to the Lake Champlain lowlands. In fact, the first railroad in the state was built along the White River, in the 1840s, and for the next hundred years White River Junction was a thriving railroad town, with freight yards, roundhouses, and thirty-five daily passenger trains. Now those thirty-five passenger trains have dwindled to just two, one northbound and one southbound, and the railroads themselves are paralleled by interstate highways — I-91 in the Connecticut and I-89 in the White River valleys. Long freights still rumble through White River Junction in the middle of the night, but most of the town's activity has shifted away from the depot to the cluster of motels and gas stations out by the interstate exits.

Railroads were important in their day, but it was the automobile that effectively brought the backwoods isolation of northern New England to an end, and automotive mobility was accepted here with no less enthusiasm than elsewhere in rural America. There are, however, still a few Vermonters alive in the 1980s who have never learned how to drive a car. John Johnson is one of them. I met him on a winter morning while I was taking pictures of trains in White River Junction and he was shoveling his driveway. He wore a railroader's blue denim coat and a red-billed hat with ear flaps. His white hair and the shape of his nose reminded me of William O. Douglas, the Supreme Court justice.

"Did you ever hear of the White River Valley Railroad?" Mr. Johnson asked me. I had. It used to run from Bethel to Rochester, and in his younger days, John Johnson worked on the line as a section hand and as a spare brakeman.

Mr. Johnson, who is four years older than Ronald Reagan, was born in Gaysville, Vermont. "I went to high school in Bethel," he said. "We went back and forth with a buggy in the summertime and a sleigh in the winter. I went to Whitcomb High School in Bethel for one year and then I had the chance to work on the railroad. I was sixteen or seventeen."

He worked on a section crew consisting of three men and a foreman. They replaced ties, raised track, checked the gauge, and cleared brush from the right of way. In the spring, they contended with washouts and sliding clay banks. Derailments might happen any time of the year. In the winter, a wing plow and a flanger cleared the main line, but all the side tracks were shoveled out by hand. To get from one job to another, the section crew had a pump car and a motor car fitted with small railroad wheels. "That was a balky critter," Mr. Johnson said. "We had to push it sometimes, but when it went it made a lot of noise."

Today trackworkers wear hard hats. They operate heavy equipment and check the alignment of the rails with laser beams. In the 1920s, everything was done with sledgehammers, crowbars, jacks, and shovels. "We used to go to the gravel pit in Bethel," Mr. Johnson said. "The engine would back two big ballast cars in there and we'd load them up. It was kind of like a day off because when the cars were full, we could go to the pool hall or one thing or another. That's the only time in my life the sun ever got to me. I figured the sooner we finished the sooner we could go over to town, so I went at it like a bull to a gate. After a while my brother says to me, 'You know John, there's three other fellows here besides you. You ain't got to load this gravel all by yourself.' "

Then, as now, the railroad paid better than average wages: a regular section hand made $4 a day. But most men in the White River Valley, whether they worked on the railroad, in the quarries, or in a woodworking mill, also took on a variety of odd jobs during the course of a year. Some cut cordwood or helped out haying. Others paid off their taxes with roadwork. And just about every family had some kind of part-time agricultural enterprise going on the side.

"We always had cows," Mr. Johnson said, "even after we came down here to White River Junction. Not any great amount, but always two or three. We'd plan it so one would come in in the spring and another in the fall, and that way my wife could make butter and sell it around, here and there. I paid for a cow once by letting the fellow who loaned me the money have two pounds of butter a week. It took awhile, but we squared it off. We always had some hens and one time we had some goats. We had a nice little herd of goats. My dad always had horses. He was a teamster and he worked for the railroad on and off too.

My oldest brother drove one team and my dad drove the other. For years my brother went around to the dairy farms picking up cream."

Tourists came to the White River Valley even in those days. Mr. Johnson remembered a family who rented a house in Gaysville: "Their name was Poor, but they weren't poor at all. They drove up in a great big Franklin motor car with a chauffeur. Then there was this single woman. She was an old maid, or at least that's what I figured. She painted pictures, and I guess she was an artist. She'd stay on from June up through September."

The great flood of 1927 nearly wiped out the White River Valley Railroad. It was rebuilt, then abandoned a few years later during the Depression. John Johnson saw the end coming.

"I got a job in a woodworking mill," he told me, "but my dad and my brother and a lot of other fellows around town helped take the railroad up." Then he hired out with the Central Vermont Railway. "We started out in one of the most dismal spots in the world," he told me, "up to Braintree." Braintree, Vermont, is a small village near the headwaters of the Third Branch of the White River. "I was with the spare gang," he said. "We lived in those boarding cars. John Morrel's wife was the head cook, and she had a man cook and a cookee. They put out the food in good shape. I bet there were a hundred and twenty-five men in that crew." The Central Vermont Railway still survives as a subsidiary of the vast Canadian National system.

The 1927 flood was the worst in the history of Vermont. A certain amount of flooding is to be expected on all rivers; there is nothing freakish about it. Floods recharge groundwater supplies and renew stream habitat. The fertility of alluvial bottom-land soil depends on periodic flooding. But in addition to the annual small floods that occur during the spring freshet, there have been at least twenty major floods in Vermont since 1770. Some were given names, such as the Jefferson Flood of 1801, the Nebraska Flood of 1854, and the Pumpkin Freshet of 1869. The flood of 1936 was the "flood of record" — the highest known water levels — for the Connecticut Valley as a whole. Railroads washed out, factories filled with water, and hundreds of communities were evacuated. Barns, houses, and dead cattle came drifting down stream on the swollen current, and a major ice jam formed at Holyoke. Hartford was placed under martial law, and Coast Guard rescue boats cruised the streets of Northampton, Massachusetts. Just two years later, in the fall of 1938, a hurricane struck the New England coast, and the accompanying rains caused severe floods in Connecticut. I remember the hurricane and flood of 1955. The power was out in West Hartford and we cooked meals in the living room fireplace. Five thousand people were injured and property damage totaled $800 million.

In Vermont, it was the November 1927 flood that caused the worst damage. Ten inches of rain fell during a thirty-six-hour period in the central part of the state. The White River became a torrent the like of which had never been seen before. At its peak, the flow approached 120,000 cubic feet per second, ninety times the normal rate. The Central Vermont Railway sustained heavy damage, and the White River Valley Railroad was completely destroyed.

"Everything but the bridges went out," Mr. Johnson told me. "George Stephenson was the roadmaster. He knew how to build a good bridge." Elsewhere in the valley, and all across the state, some twelve hundred highway and railroad bridges were wiped out. Eighty-five people were killed. Property damage came to $35 million — in an era when John Johnson had bought a house, a barn, and ten acres of land for $600. The town of Gaysville, Vermont, on a particularly dangerous stretch of the White River, was virtually obliterated. "Before" and "after" photographs tell the story. The first picture shows a typical rural village; the second, what appears to be a raw gravel pit.

The flood was an adventure for some, a test of biblical proportions for others. Afterward, flood pictures were carefully, almost lovingly, preserved in family albums, and towns published commemorative booklets. The enthusiasm for floods, however, did not include a desire to have more of them, and thoughtful people began looking into the idea of flood control. The timing couldn't have been better, since the federal government was gearing up to enter its "big dam period." Two years earlier, the Army Corps of Engineers had completed a great dam at Muscle Shoals, Alabama, on the Tennessee River, and in 1928 Calvin Coolidge authorized Boulder Dam on the Colorado. The Tennessee Valley Authority was created in 1933.

The government was willing to take care of flood control in New England, but more than a few Yankees were suspicious. Were any strings attached? Would there be big electric power projects? Would the government try to set up a TVA-style empire in the Connecticut Valley? Then there was the fact that most of the benefits of flood control went to downstream cities, whereas the dams themselves would be built on rural tributaries. The closer people live to a proposed dam site the less they liked it, and who could blame them? A dam ruined good bottomland. It removed property from the tax rolls. It put people off homesteads that their families had occupied for generations.

So the bickering went on. Nevertheless, the Army Corps of Engineers completed sixteen dams on nine of the Connecticut's tributaries as well as massive dikes and flood walls in seven major downstream cities. The city of Hartford installed further protection on its own. But memories of the big floods have faded now, and it is highly unlikely that any of the seven additional dams still on the drawing board (including one for the White River in Gaysville) will be built in the foreseeable future. Attitudes against dams have hardened. Flood control attention has turned to bank stabilization, channel modification, and various "nonstructural" measures such as evacuation plans, flood warning networks, floodplain delineation studies, soil conservation projects, flood insurance, and floodplain zoning. In North Stratford, New Hampshire, a town on the upper Connecticut that is subjected to ice jam flooding nearly every year, a number of buildings were actually torn down or moved out of the danger zone. Elsewhere, however, construction continues in the middle of notorious flood areas. The Upper Valley Shopping Plaza in West Lebanon is a good example.

Nonstructural measures, properly applied, can do much to minimize damage, but they do not prevent floods. In the White River valley, no flood control dam stands in the way of the next deluge, and there *will* be another major flood.* It may not be as bad as 1927's, or it may be worse, but it will come, and people seem to be willing to live with the threat. After all, as terrible as the last flood was, it did not bring about the end of the world. You can drive through the valley today and see hundreds of houses that were built well before 1927. (And the areas hardest hit in 1927, such as Gaysville, have not been extensively rebuilt.)

In the final analysis, there is no way to prevent a certain amount of flood damage in a mountainous region like northern New England. If you move people and buildings off the floodplains, where do you put them? It is the valleys and the floodplains that make northern New England inhabitable. The valleys provide the mill seats, routes for railroads and highways, and good bottomland for agriculture. The price is periodic flooding. The rivers give, and they take away.

ॐ

With three main branches and a watershed of 709 square miles, the White River is the Connecticut's second largest tributary in terms of its drainage area. The Chicopee is the largest, and the West, Deerfield, and Farmington rivers are nearly the size of the White. The Sugar, Millers, Black, and a score of others are somewhat smaller. Then there are a host of little streams such as Cold

---

*Flooding on the White and Connecticut rivers in May 1984 was the most severe in twenty years but was no match for 1927.

River and Saxtons River, on down to the tiniest brook. To be more precise, streams can be ranked according to their order. A stream with no tributaries is a first-order stream. A stream with one or more first-order tributaries is a second-order stream, and a stream with one or more second-order tributaries is a third-order stream. Judging from the U.S. Geological Survey's topographical map, the branches of the White River are fourth-order streams, which would make the White itself a fifth-order stream, and the Connecticut a sixth-order stream. The Mississippi is a tenth-order stream; the Amazon, a thirteenth-order stream.

Apart from size and length, one thing that distinguishes a river like the Connecticut from the great rivers of the world is that the great rivers have great tributaries. The Mississippi, for example, has two colossal tributaries, the Missouri and the Ohio, with rates of flow as great or greater than that of the master stream when they converge. On the Connecticut, all the tributaries are tiny compared to the master stream. The average flow of the White River is about 1,200 cubic feet per second; the average flow of the Connecticut at its confluence with the White is 7,200 cfs.

The mountainous terrain ensures that all the tributaries of the Connecticut are short, fast-running, and steep, but since the Green Mountains are older than the White Mountains, the Vermont tributaries tend to have larger watersheds and slightly gentler gradients than those in New Hampshire. I hesitate to make too many generalizations, however, because each tributary of the Connecticut has a distinct character, due both to natural and manmade factors. The valley of the White River, for instance, is heavy on rustic traits and light on industrial development, and the flow is unhindered by dams, at least on the main stem. The water in the White River, although exceptionally clear, has a distinctive green cast to it that seems to be specific to this one stream; I have seen it nowhere else. But in the spring the White is neither clear nor green; it turns murky with runoff. I was driving along the lower White River one evening in early May, after a week of heavy rain, and the water was the color of wet cement. Normally timid little riffles had become raging rapids. I stopped the car by the bridge in West Hartford, Vermont, and got out just as two kayaks came shooting around a bend. They paused at the start of some heavy waves, then one of the boats came ahead, promptly skidded off the side of a big roller and flipped over, then drifted into an eddy. I waited for the kayak to pop back up again, as I had seen boats do on the West River, and when it didn't I began to wonder if the paddler was hurt. Finally he surfaced and swam his kayak to shore. As he climbed up the bank, the spray cover from the kayak dangled around his waist like a little black skirt, and his bare legs were bright red from the frigid water.

In the summer the White River gentles down. Most of the rapids vanish, and at numerous places along its lower course it flows transparently over outcroppings of horizontally stratified bands of dark green rock. The current has long since rounded off all the sharp edges, hollowed out deep pools, and built up sand beaches. A phenomenal number of crayfish live in the White River along with trout, walleyes, schools of big suckers, and snapping turtles. There are resident ospreys, kingfishers, nesting mergansers, and minks that prowl the banks. The White and its side streams are also prime salmon-spawning habitat, the best in the Connecticut watershed, and there is a large federal salmon hatchery in Bethel.

∾

Peter Dunning and I set out to see the White River valley for ourselves on May 14, 1983, a Saturday. Getting Peter to tear himself away from the farm — to waste an entire afternoon on fun — was not easy, but a cold, sodden spring had pushed back the planting season and left him with some time on his hands. The chilly weather had even interfered with the sheep shearing, for cold sheep have to be warmed up (by crowding the animals together in a pen) before you can put the clippers to them. But rainy spells bring good canoeing. By my guess, the White was running 3,500 to 4,000 cubic feet per second, and Saturday turned out to be clear and sunny. Peter's frustration evaporated as we drove up the valley. The trees were leafing and the rain-washed air sparkled. Near South Royalton, Peter pointed out the house of a dairy equipment repairman who had once traded a Surge milking machine for one of Peter's border collies. When we crossed to the other side of the river, we found a good put-in spot.

The current was brisk and the water silty, but I could dimly see the bottom stones racing along under the canoe as we accelerated into the first set of riffles. Seconds later, a duck took off downstream.

"Merganser," I said.

"With all that white on it?" Peter said. Well, I told him, if I hadn't learned anything else on the river, I knew how to spot a merganser by now. Another noisy riffle was coming up. I stood in the stern for a better view but couldn't see much, one route looking as good as another. We shot over the lip of a ledge on a smooth cushion of high-speed water and bounced through the zone of waves below it, zigzagging around rocks. Canoes were made for rivers like this.

The riffles seemed to come in bunches, three or four to the mile, and then there would be a mile or so of smooth water, but always with a good current, perhaps 7 or 8 miles per hour. Paddling was optional except to maneuver. It is characteristic of the lower White to have ledges running all the way across the riverbed at the sharper drops. Often a narrow break in the ledge will admit a canoe, but these passages can be difficult to spot. At a high water level it is easier to scoot right over the top. The main thing is to avoid coming down on a rock.

A paved highway runs along the river, sometimes by the bank, sometimes at a distance. Interstate 89 and the Central Vermont Railway are present, too, first on one side of the valley and then on the other, but neither the railroad nor the highway is visible for more than a few minutes at a stretch, and the noise of the riffles smothers the traffic sounds. There were quantities of driftwood all along the shore, and good-size trees had been pulled up by their roots and left stranded on the islands.

The miles sped by. Each time Peter and I began a conversation another set of riffles would divert us, and presently the town of Sharon came into view. The Mormon leader Joseph Smith was born back up in the hills near Sharon, although the Smith family, like so many others in Vermont, emigrated to western New York in the nineteenth century; young Joseph was fourteen at the time. Below Sharon, the river tumbles over ledges to enter a long, twisting gorge, and once we were in it I began to hear a roaring noise. Peter turned around in the bow and looked at me, a grin on his face. The roar got louder and louder, and some old bridge abutments appeared in the distance. The closer we got to them, the more they looked like the remains of a broken dam, which is what they are. The dam must have washed out in the 1927 flood.

We beached the canoe and walked along the bank to take a look. There was an easy portage on the far side of the river, but it seemed as though the dam could be run on the right. Peter thought we could do it. I wasn't convinced. Jagged chunks of concrete littered the riverbed, and I was worried about the keeper wave just below the drop, but Peter said he could move back against the center thwart to lighten the bow.

We put on our life jackets and shoved off. I felt a powerful surge at the lip; there was a brief instant of weightlessness before the canoe tilted downhill and punched through the keeper, engulfed in spray. I wiped the water from my face and suddenly the roar of the dam was loud in my ears again. I hadn't been aware of any sound at all when the canoe went over the edge. We drifted on down to a Central Vermont Railway bridge.

"Nineteen twenty-eight," said Peter, reading the numerals

carved into one of the concrete piers. The year 1928 was a big one for bridge building in Vermont. There were rusty steel girders, bent and twisted like paper clips, on the bottom of the river, then rapids ahead. I aimed the canoe diagonally across the current and leaned way out on my paddle as we came to a ledge, making the bow pivot downstream to avoid a rock. We bounced through haystacks and swerved around boulders. The rapids seemed to be getting bigger. I wanted to stop and empty the water that was sloshing in the bottom of the canoe, but there wasn't time. Another rapid was coming up. I saw a clear channel off to one side, but Peter dismissed it. He wanted more whitewater. We shot straight down the middle, rocketing over two ledges in quick succession; then, before I had a chance even to think about reacting, a big wave broke over the gunwale, heavy and solid. I watched it with that horribly detailed slow-motion vision, noticing the bubbles and the whiteness of the foam as the canoe filled and rolled over. I never went all the way under, but Peter was nowhere in sight. Then he popped up on the other side of the boat. We were now racing downstream at 7 miles per hour (which may not sound fast, but it is). The banks seemed to go by in a blur. I hadn't oriented myself yet. I was just letting it happen, glancing off rocks without trying to avoid them. Foolishly, we had shed our life jackets after the dam. My rubber-bottom shoe pacs each felt as if they weighed 50 pounds. I knew I wasn't going to drown, but I was getting tired. Peter and I both tried to grab the canoe, but it kept rolling over and over. Filled with water, it was completely unmanageable. I had no idea how we were going to get it to shore. The current was incredibly powerful. Then Peter spotted his paddle and I reached out and caught it.

Peter seemed more concerned about the canoe than I was. I wouldn't have blamed him if he had just tried to get himself out of the river. The water wasn't as cold as I had expected, but perhaps that was due to the excitement. It would get a lot colder if we didn't do something soon. I could hear another rapid ahead, and it proved to be a godsend. We fetched up on a big rock — big enough to stand on — and we were able to empty most of the water out of the canoe. Somewhat incredibly, my paddle and both life jackets were still inside the hull.

My watch had stopped dead, pinpointing the time of the spill at 2:32 P.M., but I still had my wallet, pocket knife, and car keys. The sun had already begun to take the chill off, and both of us were starting to feel pretty good about the whole thing. It had been fun, in a way. You wouldn't want to dump a canoe on purpose, but it was certainly an excellent object lesson in the power of moving water. Three or four rapids later we came to the West Hartford bridge and dragged the canoe up the bank.

❧

Below West Hartford, the White River is smooth for a while and then drops over ledges, becoming quite wide and shallow in spots and providing a superior place to practice poling. I did this stretch on May 18 and enjoyed a fast ride through jittery green waves to the flatwater under the I-91 high bridge in White River Junction. A half-mile later I passed under three more bridges and came to a small municipal park on the triangular point of land where the White flows into the Connecticut.

This part of the Connecticut, from Wilder Dam 1 mile north to Sumner Falls 5 miles south, will freeze in very cold weather, but it usually stays open because of an exceptionally strong current, due in part to releases of water from the dam, although I suspect that this has always been a fast stretch of river. Any doubts about the current's speed are banished once you see the ice racing downstream. I like to watch it, and apparently it fascinates crows as well. I once observed a noisy flock that had assembled in a tree by the river not far from Sumner Falls. Two or three crows at a time would glide out and land on a piece of ice, riding it downstream to the beginning of the rapids before returning to their excited companions.

When enough ice comes down the river it jams at the falls, piling up into a towering jumble of blocks that reaches from bank to bank. The main drop at Sumner Falls is only about 10 feet, but aside from Enfield Rapids and some cascades in the headwaters region, this is the last significant set of falls on the Connecticut that have not been drowned, dried up, or otherwise adulterated by a dam. I first saw Sumner Falls on a rainy day during a December warm spell, and the amount of effort that went into the visit increased my appreciation. I began by driving along a back road on the New Hampshire side of the river, searching for a place to carry the canoe down through the woods to the water. Suddenly a small bird flew across the path of the car and glanced off the windshield. I stopped and found the bird, a chickadee, lying in the wet dirt. It had no visible injuries but must have been broken up pretty badly inside. It just lay there, opening and closing its beak, not making a sound. When I picked it up it seemed to have no weight at all, and I was struck by its minute perfection: tiny brown eyes with black pupils, and a delicate flush of pale golden feathers across the white breast. I broke its neck and tossed it into a stubble field.

The river seemed low, but apparently it was rising. It made a soft whooshing sound as it swept over the partially exposed gravel bars. Patchy white fog hung above the water. I stuck to the shallows, where I could use the pole, and made fairly good progress until I ran up against a big birch tree that had fallen out from the bank. I got past it by climbing onto the trunk and pulling the canoe underneath. There were other trees ahead. In the rain, the river was a cool gray-green, and the slick gravel bars were wet and shiny. The murmur of the riffles was continual. Ducks flew overhead from time to time, their wings making a wonderful whistling sound. The showers came down in spurts, with drizzle in between, the white mist thickening as the rain let up and dissipating when it began again. Before long I stopped noticing whether it was raining or not. The river was wide and fast, a totally absorbing challenge. If I had been more skillful with the pole it wouldn't have been difficult at all, but I wasn't, and I was working up a sweat inside my slicker.

Eventually I came to a slack current, where the river spread out into a large pool at the foot of the falls. I could hear the roar up ahead, around a bend, and then I was engulfed in a sudden, torrential downpour. The driving rain hissed and spit on the surface of the river like hot grease on a skillet. I cruised upstream until the falls came into sight. The main drop was split in two by a rocky island, with creamy water tumbling down either side, frothing in the eddies below.

The rain ended as abruptly as it had begun, and the mist started to roll back in. Drawing closer to the falls, I was surprised to see a car parked on the Vermont side. Never having been there before, I didn't realize that you can drive down to the river on an unmarked dirt road. A fisherman in an olive-drab poncho and a red hat stood on a rock, casting. He said the walleyes were running. When Major Robert Rogers came down the river in 1759, this spot was known as Wattockquitchey Falls. Having met disaster in rapids already, Rogers attached his raft to a rope made of vines and had his three companions lower the craft through the whitewater as best they could from the shore. The raft got away from them, but Rogers, who was waiting at the bottom of the falls, dove in and saved it.

Sumner Falls presented an impassable barrier to flatboats, and a short canal was dug on the Vermont side in the early 1800s. There was a sawmill as well, but a flood washed it away, and few traces of either the mill or the canal remain. I did find, however, one of the small bronze disks placed by the Supreme Court in 1936 to mark the Vermont–New Hampshire border. A little farther inland, up in the woods on a bluff, I came across a slate gravestone with this inscription:

JOHN A. BARBER
DIED 1895
AGE 19
CHERRYFIELD, MAINE

I found out later that he had been killed on a log drive, most likely when the logs jammed in the rapids, and that none of his relatives were willing to pay to have the body shipped home.

The falls are at their most impressive in the spring, right after the ice goes out, but by August the flow may dwindle down to a trickle, especially while Wilder Dam is storing water. Somewhere between those extremes the rapids are a fine playground for kayaks and an exciting, albeit short, run for expert canoeists. Linda Hay once told me she saw a man get out of a kayak here with a full-length cast on one leg. At a very low water level it is even possible to pole a canoe *up* the falls. I like to remember Sumner Falls as they were on my first visit, in the mist and the rain. I stood by the log driver's grave and let my mind run back to the wild river, trying to conjure up a vision of leaping salmon and fishing eagles; after a while I got back in the canoe and went out to the midstream island. The mist was thickening again, obscuring the shore, softening and erasing everything except the roaring rapids. In the dim light the water was jet black, like polished marble, until it broke on the rocks, erupting into spray. I closed my eyes and listened to the pounding thunder of the falls, letting the noise well up inside my head until it began to take on different colors, soothing and powerful at the same time, a pure distillation of the river spirit, of riverhood itself.

That was December; now it was May. I was heading upstream, and a man standing in the park at the mouth of the White River stared at me as I went by. Anyone in a boat is a legitimate object of curiosity — you can't take offense — but this fellow really gave me the eyeball. And I didn't like the cut of his leisure suit. His wife had a little white dog on a leash. The man looked at me as though he had never seen a canoe before.

It was only a little more than a mile to Wilder Dam, but with the strong current it took over an hour. There is a sharp drop in the riverbed at Wilder, and there used to be rapids here, White River Falls by name, sometimes called Olcott Falls. This is where Rogers lost his first raft in 1759. The men swam to shore when they saw what was about to happen, but the raft was completely destroyed.

As at Sumner Falls, a flatboat canal was dug around the rapids in the early 1800s. A large paper mill was later built on the Vermont side, but it closed in 1915. The present NEPCO dam, with a gross head of 53 feet and a spillway elevation of 383 feet above sea level, was built in 1950. The dam does not have a fish ladder yet, although one is planned. The ladder at Vernon is fully operational, and the new $8.1 million ladder at Bellows Falls was opened in the spring of 1984. A man from the Bethel hatchery told me that in 1982, forty large salmon were caught in special traps below the Bellows Falls Dam and carried to the pond above.

It was dams, of course, both on the tributaries and on the master stream, that brought the great Connecticut River salmon runs to an end in the late 1700s, despite public outcry. Still, it seems utterly inconceivable that the dams could ever have been prohibited — the New England industrial revolution would have been very different without them — and now it is entirely appropriate that the money earned from water power, in the form of contributions by companies such as NEPCO and Northeast Utilities, will defray at least part of the tremendous cost of the salmon restoration project. It is an article of faith that the salmon are worth this, and people devote themselves to the cause with a religious zeal that is not entirely explained by the Atlantic salmon's stature as the most glamorous game fish in the world. It is, I think, not so much the salmon itself as the things that the presence of salmon imply — clean water, free-flowing streams, wildness — that excite such fervor. And the salmon *are* magnificent. A salmon is wildness you can see, wildness you can touch; it is riverhood, just as the thunder of the rapids at Sumner Falls is riverhood, a thing so fine and pure as to be beyond any price.

అ

The Wilder Pond is exceptionally long, extending upstream for some 45 miles, but like the pond behind the Bellows Falls Dam, it looks more like a river than a lake. On the evening of May 25 I launched the canoe at North Thetford, Vermont, about 20 miles above White River Junction. Clouds had moved in with the afternoon, but the night air was balmy, without the slightest trace of wind, and the surface of the water made a perfect mirror to the sky, marred only by patches of floating dandelion fluff. The weak current was just barely detectable, and the water seemed almost warm to the touch. It felt denser than normal, as if it had been laced with syrup. I concentrated on silent paddling.

Exhaust fans hummed in a dairy barn on the New Hampshire side. Someone roared away in a blue Camaro, making the tires smoke. Small fish were jumping, and swallows darted back and forth in the dusk, chattering as they hovered in front of their burrows in the bank. The silky water seemed to cry out for speed, and I could not resist starting the motor. I skimmed upstream, leaving a broad, rolling wake that lapped on the shore. The river in front of me was wide and placid in the dying light. The motor blocked out all other noise, but after a while I saw a big splash that could only have been caused by a beaver sliding down the bank. Then I saw the beaver's head coming straight toward me, and I shut off the motor. The beaver began a frenzy of tail slapping, gradually leading me to his lodge. I would never have noticed it if he hadn't made such a fuss. Loud tail slaps erupted on both sides of the canoe. There were at least two beavers out there, a big fellow who swam around with his head pointed stiffly upward and a smaller animal who kept his distance.

Off to the east a full moon had risen above the trees, blurred and orange behind thin clouds, like a flashlight shining through a wool blanket. The frogs and peepers had started in, and a mosquito bit me on the wrist. It was getting cool enough for a jacket. I stood up in the canoe and saw a lonely pole light next to a silo, far across a black sweep of bottomland. Closer to the river, three or four lighted windows showed through the trees at widely spaced intervals. Mostly it was dark.

The flatboats used to tie up at night. The crew slept on board, if the boat had a cabin, or stayed in a riverside tavern. It was physical exhaustion, not a lack of visibility, that ruled out nocturnal navigation. I could see just fine. The moon had risen above the clouds and cast a cold, strong light, sufficient to make shadows. Perhaps you wouldn't want to run a rapid in the moonlight, but you probably could. I couldn't help thinking back to the January night on the tugboat when we came up the river breaking ice. Even in a driving snowstorm the visibility had been adequate.

I remembered the steady throb of the tug's diesels and the rumble of the ice against the hull. Now, in May, the canoe slipped through the water without making any noise at all. I let it drift for a while and listened to a whippoorwill calling in the woods. A hermit thrush tried a few notes and quit. For a moment I thought I saw a bat. Stars pricked through the clouds dimly, and the sound of a train came floating down the valley, fading in and out but growing louder. The track runs along the Vermont bank, and I noticed that a block signal had flicked on, the green beam of light reflecting in the water. In due course the train rolled by, the locomotive's headlight cutting a brilliant swath through the darkness; after it was gone the block signal was red. Then it went out.

I could still hear the train blowing for grade crossings way down the line — two long hoots, a short, and a long — becoming fainter and fainter. A dog barked, then stopped, and everything was quiet until the whippoorwill started again. My wet paddle blade glistened in the moonlight.

11 ❧ THETFORD

to BARNET

The Upper Valley

*I*N 1759 IT TOOK Robert Rogers less than a day and a half to float down the Connecticut from the mouth of the Ammonoosuc River to Olcott Falls (the site of the present Wilder Dam), and he did it in a crude log raft, using sticks for paddles. A canoe would have made even better time. Today, however, the current is slack because of the 45-mile pond, and a raft journey like Rogers' might take three or four days — if you did not encounter a headwind. But while the loss of the free-flowing river is regrettable, the Upper Valley is still an extraordinarily beautiful place. The first time I drove through here, perhaps a dozen years ago, I could barely keep the car on the road. This is country with a hidden power in it, a flow of strong, pure emotion that runs deep. It comes over you like something you have always known instinctively but never tried to remember. It is peaceful and green and majestic, brimming over with the slow wisdom of woods and fields, the shimmering clarity of open spaces, and the solid heft of old mountains.

The mountains get bigger up here, rising in dense, choppy waves to the wind-blasted climax of Mount Washington and the Presidential Range, but visible only now and then in quick glimpses, through gaps in the foothills, until suddenly Mount Moosilauke looms above the eastern rim of the valley, filling the sky, stern and aloof and very close, like the bulging crest in a wall of thunderheads. The Connecticut's floodplain begins to widen, and the bottomland is intensively cultivated as the river meanders in broad loops. It is the finest pastoral landscape I have ever seen.

This reach of valley, with its fertile alluvial soil and naturally open meadows, was long used by the Indians as a place to plant corn. They called it the Coos Country. It was attractive to white homesteaders, too, who leapfrogged up here from Charlestown, bypassing areas to the south, as soon as the French and Indian wars were over. Most of the towns sit up on terraces deposited by the glacial melt lake, usually where a tributary stream tumbles down to the valley floor, to take advantage of the water power. Such is the case with Bradford, Vermont, on the little Waits River,* about 15 miles north of Thetford. Bradford looks out across the Connecticut Valley to the village of Piermont, New Hampshire — on another terrace — with Mount Moosilauke rising in the distance. The old dam on the Waits has been completely rebuilt by the Central Vermont Public Service Company to generate 1½ megawatts.

I launched the canoe below the dam on June 15 at the state boat ramp in the Bradford fairgrounds. The cool morning fog had just about burned off, and it looked as if another scorcher was on the way, the heat already hanging in the air, thick and heavy, like a steaming towel. Thunderstorms were predicted for the afternoon. A persistent yellowjacket buzzed around my legs, and a gospel revival meeting was setting up shop nearby, bright-eyed young men unloading folding chairs from a truck. I

*Named after one of Rogers' Rangers, who shot a deer nearby.

shoved off. The water in the Waits River was clear and shallow and fast, the current tumbling twigs and sticks along the firm, sandy bottom as the channel meandered across pastureland and then into a marsh. Pigeons on the B&M bridge cooed as the canoe slipped silently underneath the rusty truss span. A green heron flew off into the trees, and the shrill, penetrating call of a killdeer carried over the cattails. It is a sound that always makes me think of March and April, for killdeer are among the first birds to arrive in the spring. You see them in pairs, in thawing fields or along the rivers just after ice-out, unmistakable with their snowy, black-barred breast and their bobbing, jittery walk as they pick around the big blocks of dirty ice cast up on the banks.

It's always a little sad to see the runoff come to an end — the freshet is a river's finest hour — but this year a rainy spring had prolonged the whitewater canoe season. In fact, Peter Dunning and I had a fine run on the Sugar River from Newport to Claremont in the beginning of June. The part I am thinking of drops 40 feet to the mile for several miles in one stretch, producing continuous rapids. Frequent Class II and Class III pitches demand precise maneuvering, but without the adrenaline-pumping, boat-crunching hydraulics of big water (although we did find the shattered bow of a fiberglass canoe bobbing in an eddy below Sweet Tooth Rapids). The scenery was wild and lonely — only the abandoned right of way of the old Claremont & Concord Railway comes close to the banks — but we were going too fast to take much of it in, dodging rocks and punching through waves. I have never enjoyed myself in a canoe quite so much.

But the high water was gone. When the weather turned hot, the river seemed to drop overnight. Rapids became gentle riffles and riffles became bone-dry gravel bars, baking in the sun. The change was less abrupt on the Connecticut because dams control so much of the flow, but the water level had fallen nevertheless. This morning, as I drifted out the mouth of the

Waits River and turned up the Connecticut, a foot or two of slick mud was showing below the normal vegetation line on the banks. The glassy water still retained some of its early morning black color, and the sun's reflection gleamed on the surface a few inches from the right gunwale, moving along with me as I paddled. Silver-bright droplets draining off the paddle blade lingered on top of the water for a second, like tiny balls of mercury from a broken thermometer, before disappearing. The leaves on the trees were absolutely still.

About 2 miles upstream, a man in the air-conditioned cab of a big tractor was chopping haylage, going back and forth across a field. The railroad had appeared over on the Vermont bank, at milepost 153, and I noticed a block signal mounted on an extra-tall mast (because of a curve). The signal's days were numbered since the entire system was being dismantled north of White River Junction. Block signals guard against rear-end and head-on collisions, but with only three or four slow freights using the line each day, such precautions were no longer necessary.

The inside of meandering curves along this reach of river often have inviting sandy beaches, and I ran the canoe up on one of them to write some things in my notebook, scattering the cows that had come down to drink. A few minutes later they began to drift back — twenty-five or thirty of them — crowding all around, snorting and craning their necks, urinating nervously in the sand in long, loud streams. I rapped the gunwale with the setting pole and went back to writing. Then I felt a sandpaper tongue on the back of my neck. Other cows were licking the side of the hull. Perhaps it was salty. Gradually the cows nudged the canoe out into the river.

There were deer tracks on the beaches, too, dainty compared to those of the cows, and when I came to a shallow pool partially closed off by a sandbar, two vultures that had been sitting on an old stump rose into the air, big and black, like sudden chilly shadows across the sun, their 6-foot wings flapping slowly and heavily with a barely audible whooshing sound. The birds gained altitude and commenced to soar, sailing off until they were specks. Vultures like the air currents above the valley; they can cruise effortlessly all day in endless wheeling arcs, inspecting the fields.

Faint wakes trailing from the branches of a tree that had fallen into the river proved that there actually is a current here. Although slight, it makes a difference to a paddler over the course of several hours. I switched back and forth from poling to paddling whenever I started to get tired. The two techniques are different enough so that the change was almost like taking a rest. (You can see more, however, when you stand up to use the pole.) The water was clear in the shallows and populated with schools of minnows, an occasional large bass or pike, and swift fleets of boat-shaped beetles swimming on the surface. There were dozens of narrow furrows in the mud, about 10 or 15 feet long, each leading to a clam. Peeled beaver sticks floated in the river, some with green leaves still attached. Poplar and birch are scarce along here; the Coos Country beavers resort to silver maple or even to cornstalks on occasion. Milky heat haze obscured the mountains, and a slight breeze had begun to stir, bringing the hot land smell with it. I paused frequently to take quick dips, but the water was frigid, making my legs ache while I gathered the nerve to go all the way in. It takes a long time for the Connecticut to warm up.

About one o'clock, a bend in the river revealed the old Bedel Bridge site. Nothing is left now save a midstream pier and the abutments on either bank. The bridge, a Burr truss wooden covered span, blew down in a high wind in 1979, just a few months after volunteers had completed a six-year restoration project. There are four surviving covered bridges across the Connecticut, including a 460-foot two-span Burr truss between Windsor, Vermont, and Cornish, New Hampshire, the longest covered bridge in the United States. It's a tough old bridge that withstood countless ice jams and runaway log drives, one of which destroyed a steel railroad bridge immediately down-stream, but age (117 years) and traffic (1,700 cars a day) have taken their toll. The east span has a pronounced sag, and major work is scheduled to be done. Vermont will pay for part of it, even though the bridge is New Hampshire's responsibility.

A few miles above the Bedel Bridge the current began to increase a little, which is to be expected near the head of the pond. Wilder Dam was now some 35 miles downstream. Sun-light winked on the stainless steel tank of a milk truck making a pickup at a dairy barn up on a terrace in Haverhill, New Hampshire, way across a flat sweep of bottomland. Three trac-tors, one pulling a disk harrow, the other two hitched to corn planters, worked in the fields on the Vermont side. Gulls fol-lowed the harrow. It was late for planting corn; the soil here must have taken a long time to dry out. Hydrologists call this part of the valley a natural storage area. Floodwaters collect here in broad, shallow lakes after a heavy rain.

Just around the next bend I caught sight of the Newbury–North Haverhill highway bridge, my destination. I never dreamed it was so close. Now I had the rest of the afternoon for a lazy float back downstream to Bradford.

⟡

June 23. I drove up the valley in the morning and backed the car down the steep boat ramp by the Newbury Bridge. It was eight A.M. and hot, but without the oppressive humidity of the previous couple of weeks. In between commercials for milking machines and manure spreaders, the weather forecast on the radio station in Wells River, Vermont, said it would be a good day to dry hay. The temperature was supposed to get up into the nineties. The river had fallen 6 inches since I had been here, according to the painted depth gauge on one of the bridge piers.

I had to shove the canoe through oozy black mud at the foot of the ramp to get to the water.

If you drive across the bridge to New Hampshire and turn right at the top of the hill, you come to the North Haverhill fairgrounds. The parking lot would be empty today, but it was jammed last July when I went to the fair on a sweltering Saturday morning. The midway was a dusty swirl of shuffling feet, blinking light bulbs, and blaring loudspeakers. I paused to inspect the big white dish of a satellite earth station, then looked at some shiny New Holland balers and a mammoth, comfort-cab John Deere tractor that resembled some formidable species of bright green metal insect, the padded black Naugahyde driver's seat still wrapped in clear plastic, fresh from the factory in Moline, Illinois. Inside the concession tents I discovered dairy equipment, microwave ovens, rolls of wall-to-wall carpet, gas-oline-powered log splitters, motorcycles, sewing machines, and electric living room organs. Cosmetics, jewelry, soil conservation district pamphlets, and brass belt buckles shaped like bulldozers and crossed chain saws were laid out on card tables. The show barns had vegetables, pies, flower arrangements, quilts, 4-H projects, angora rabbits, calves, steers, sheep, and goats. The snowy, black-faced Hampshire sheep reminded me of inflated Siamese cats. Big pink sows with seven or eight piglets sucking at their teats drew crowds.

Most fairgoers spent at least a few minutes watching the ox pull. The pace of the contest is slow and methodical; concrete blocks are placed on a flat metal sled called a stone boat and each yoke of oxen gets three tries — if three are needed — at moving the boat a distance of 7 feet. Then a tractor puts more blocks on the boat and the next round begins. The animals compete in weight classes, like prizefighters, with the smaller teams coming on first. Between hitches, the oxen stand stoically around the edge of the ring, their owners sitting beside them in lawn chairs.

A surprising number of horses still earn their keep in the northern New England woods on logging operations, and so do a few of the oxen, but I get the impression that oxen are kept mainly as a hobby. Some teams work the fair circuit all summer and fall, hitting a pulling event every week. For the owners it's really a labor of love, since only a modest amount of prize money is involved. Patient training of the animals is important. The oxen are controlled by voice commands, although a long springy stick with a piece of string dangling from the end is used for emphasis.

There are pulling events for horses, too, that are more exciting. Along with strength and size, the big draft horses have fire and style, which oxen lack. Oxen endure the competition; horses appear to relish it. It's the tractor pull, however, that really pleases the crowd at most country fairs, with classes for vintage tractors, stock tractors, superstocks, and modified. A "modified" tractor is definitely not something you can buy down at the neighborhood implement dealer. These exotic machines are built by hand, with long, low-slung drag-racer-type frames, tiny front wheels, gargantuan tractor tires in the rear, dazzling metal-flake paint jobs, and one or two 400-cubic-inch supercharged engines. When one of these mothers fires up, the noise is painful. Electric currents of excitement surge through the bleachers.

The atmosphere was considerably more sedate inside the dairy judging barn. It was cool and dim under the slanting metal roof, with clean sawdust on the floor, a milking parlor down at one end, and cows of all breeds in the open stalls along the walls, including impish little caramel-colored Jerseys, chocolate brown milking shorthorns, red and white Ayrshires, and huge dowager Holsteins with soulful liquid eyes and glossy black flanks. Bloodlines are hardly less important in cows than in racehorses; a champion in a major dairy show commands a six-figure price. A nine-year-old Wisconsin Holstein recently brought a record $1,025,000 at auction. But pride rather than money was on the line at the North Haverhill Fair. These cows had been raised by teenagers. Dressed in white shirts and white ducks, running shoes showing under the cuffs, they walked their animals in a circle while their parents looked on. The judge, a thin, sharp-eyed man with the earnest air of a preacher, found something nice to say about every entry and heaped praise on the winners. "Now this is a fine animal here. We like the scale of the frame, the upstandingness of it. There's plenty of conditioning — might want to take some of that off. Her udder's hitched on good forward, and high and wide in the rear. She's dairy."

Outside it was getting hotter. A pair of water trucks went slowly back and forth, sprinkling the midway and the show rings to keep the dust down. Long lines formed at the stands selling cold drinks. A special pulling event for three-horse teams in the unlimited weight class — "open to all the world" — was scheduled for seven in the evening, and the horses were being unloaded in a field beyond the parking lots. I wandered over to watch, settling down on the grass in the shade of some tall, fence-line oaks. This was more like it. Babies were asleep on blankets. Women were spreading out picnics. Men gathered in groups to talk quietly and lay hands on horseflesh. I like to watch the old-timers with their animals. One of the very first things I can remember as a small child is my grandfather sitting me up on one of his gigantic draft horses. These horses at the fair, I suspect, were even bigger. Their manes were clipped back to a stiff-looking brush, their hooves shod with chrome-plated spike shoes.

Long about four in the afternoon, the next to the last weight class of oxen entered the ring, great lumbering beasts with heavy heads and rolling lumps of muscle. The bleachers were full, and as many more people stood by the fence, squinting into the sun, hard country faces peering out from under billed caps. Despite the heat, not once all day did I see a man, or even a boy above the age of ten, in short pants.

The weight on the boat was climbing. The tantrum-prone

drivers who swear at their animals and hit them about the eyes and face had long since been eliminated. The field had narrowed down to two teams, Jake and George from Lebanon, New Hampshire, and Black Star and White Star from Fairlee, Vermont. The latter two pulled 7,250 pounds on the first hitch easily and trotted back to the fence.

The team from Lebanon, however, managed just 16 inches on their first attempt and only 9 inches on their second. The tractor winched in the boat while three men with rakes smoothed down the dirt. The weary oxen gazed off into space.

"One minute," warned the announcer, and the animals backed to hitch on for one last try.

"Back Jake! Back George!" shouted their owner. His assistant squatted down to place the hook on the end of the chain into the hole in the front of the boat; the animals, hearing it clink, set to with a will, staggering forward, frothy white spittle dribbling out of their mouths. The boat moved slowly. "All the way," said the announcer to a cheering crowd. Jake and George lost on the next round, and I went home.

Now, almost a year later, I was back — on the river, that is — with a full day of canoeing to look forward to. The first hundred or so strokes are always the hardest. It just doesn't seem possible that you can keep it up for the next ten minutes, let alone the next 10 miles. Then you get into the rhythm, and you don't want to stop. I watched the wake flow back from the bow, making thin, gradually disappearing lines. The canoe felt comfortable and slippery in the water. The varnished shaft of the paddle had a small amount of give to it; everything was just right. Three crows were mobbing a hawk, diving on the big raptor as it sat on a branch, feathers ruffled, trying to ignore its tormentors. A little later a kingbird went after the crows, chasing them off. A line of silver maples and willows ran along both banks of the river, and beyond, open fields in pasture and tillage stretched out a mile or more, east and west, to the limits of the floodplain. It was hot, the sky almost colorless, squinty in the strong morning light, but the grass was still sopping with dew, and luxuriant ferns grew in the shade.

The river began to swing around to a westerly heading, with Mount Moosilauke looming behind the stern like a dense gray cloud. It is said that two of Rogers' Rangers tried to climb Moosilauke in 1759, supposedly to help figure out where they were, but there are easier ways to obtain a view, particularly for men who were already weak with starvation. Indeed, one of the rangers died of exhaustion during the ascent. Moosilauke's summit, unlike Ascutney's, is superbly defended by a Krumholz zone, wind-stunted firs 3 or 4 feet tall packed so tightly together that you could almost walk on top of them with snowshoes. It is a bushwhacker's nightmare. But once the Krumholz is surmounted (easily, now that trails have been cut through it), the top of Moosilauke is wide-open alpine tundra, always cool and windy. The skyline diagram in the Dartmouth Outing Club guidebook — Dartmouth College now owns much of Mount Moosilauke — names 107 peaks or ranges visible in the distance, from Québec to Maine to Massachusetts to the Adirondacks in New York.

Moosilauke often holds snow well into June, but not this year. There was not even the hint of a breeze in the valley, except for what I stirred up myself. I had already stripped off my T-shirt, and sweat was beginning to trickle down the inside of my pant legs. Each time I planted the setting pole it raised a little puff of silt, then I froze at midstroke: a snapping turtle was resting on the bottom in 2 feet of water. It was a monster, with a shell like a manhole cover, thick legs, and a pointed, armored tail. A snapping turtle cannot withdraw its extremities inside its shell, and it doesn't need to. No other creature with an ounce of sense would dare to tangle with it. The evil-looking beak is warning enough. Against my better judgment, I reached out with the setting pole to see if I could provoke a response. In an instant the turtle came to life — and shot off into deep water, vanishing.

There was a dairy farm up ahead, and several more appeared as I drew nearer. The river comes close to the western edge of the floodplain here and then bends back sharply, almost reversing itself, before launching into a long gradual loop known as the Oxbow. Partway through it, six white geese came gliding downstream in formation. I put the binoculars on them and saw that a Canada goose was out in front and seemed to be the leader of this peculiar little flock. The others were big white Enden geese with orange bills and orange feet. Perhaps the Canada had lured them away from some farm pond.

The Oxbow took me way over to the eastern edge of the floodplain, then back to the west again and into another sharp curve, to the north. The same dairy farms I passed more than an hour before were close by; I had come a good 3 or 4 miles by canoe, but little more than 1 mile as the crow flies. Looking back over my shoulder I saw a red barn, the bend in the river, and Mount Moosilauke, a scene immortalized on countless postcards and plastic placemats. It is also the head of Wilder Pond. The current had been gathering strength for some time; now it became formidable.

As if to mark the spot there was a pontoon boat — most emphatically a craft for smooth waters — drawn up on shore and chained to a tree. I'm not sure that any sort of powerboat could ascend the river beyond this point, at least at the summer water level. There are too many shallow riffles, too few deep channels. The Connecticut was at last becoming a real canoe stream — a change in character that actually begins down near Windsor, Vermont, but is largely hidden by the dams — and it demanded a fine touch with the setting pole. I tried swimming here once, and as soon as I got in waist-deep the water pressed against my stomach like a high-powered Jacuzzi, almost knocking me off my feet. Now the butt of the pole tended to skid ineffectually on the hard, compacted gravel bottom unless I paid close attention.

Pools came between the riffles, as always, but the swift water went on and on. A few months earlier it would have stopped me dead; now I could make fairly good progress, but at the expense of far too much effort. Poling is infinitely perfectable. The basic poling technique is simple enough; it's getting to the point that you can do it without squandering energy that takes time and practice. I was lunging and sweating, fighting a losing battle to keep the bow lined up properly. The current simply cannot be defeated by force. It cannot be defeated at all. You have to work with it, and I still had a lot to learn. There are dozens of little tricks, all of them too subtle to describe; it's a matter of feel, of intuition, of balance, of minute course corrections and constant sensitivity to the flowing water. As it was, I had drained the water jug, and my legs were starting to shake. Then, after 4 hard miles, the green steel arch of the Woodsville bridge finally came into sight. I worked my way up one last pitch of riffles, avoiding the whitecaps out in the middle by staying near the bank, then sat down to rest in the slack water at the mouth of the Wells River, on the Vermont side. The canoe started to drift downstream and I just let it go wherever it wanted to, reaching out with the paddle now and then to steer around rocks as I bounced through the bottle-green waves.

❧

Although flatboats sometimes went up to Barnet, Vermont, the practical head of navigation on the Connecticut was Woodsville, New Hampshire, a town with a reputation for wide-open saloons and barroom brawls. One could understand, I suppose, that a man who had just poled a flatboat 200 miles against the current would be ready to raise a little hell — if, that is, he could still stand up. Flatboats had disappeared by the mid-1850s, but the river still loomed large in Woodsville's life because of lumber. Logs and lumber had long been floated down the Connect-icut in rafts, the rafts made up into "boxes," each box the size and shape of a canal lock. In the 1860s, the first of the great log drives — loose logs — began. The log drivers — or "rivermen," as they called themselves — were just as rowdy as the flatboat crews, and there were more rivermen to get into trouble. As many as five hundred accompanied a big drive. It was extremely dangerous work, and by the time the rivermen got to Woods-ville they had been wet, cold, and tired for the better part of a month. They wanted a drink, a fight, and some female compan-ionship. There is a mossy old story about an inebriated riverman who lurched down a board sidewalk in Woodsville — you could always tell where the rivermen went because their caulked boots left a distinctive mark — and plunged through a plate-glass store window to embrace a naked mannequin, clinging to it until the sheriff pulled him off.

There were also log drives on the Ammonoosuc River as well as on many of the other tributaries. With a watershed of 402 square miles, the Ammonoosuc is not gigantic, but it has a wild, rambunctious nature. Always swift, the current flashes over a clear pebble bottom and foams around huge granite boul-ders in roaring Class IV rapids — Alder Brook Rapid, Power-house Rapid, Boat Breaker Rapid, Railroad Rapid. The air smells of pine and spruce, and the valley is steep and narrow. A branch of the Boston & Maine hugs the banks, crossing from one side to the other, curving and climbing up into the mountains. And when the railroad gives up the river continues, steeper than ever, up into the clouds. The ultimate source of the Ammo-noosuc is a pair of tiny alpine tarns, the highest bodies of water in the northeastern United States, well above the treeline and just below the summit of Mount Washington itself.

The Ammonoosuc ends with a flourish, too, with a rocky set of falls at its confluence with the Connecticut in Woodsville. This, of course, was an ideal location for a dam, and a small hydroelectric unit is still in operation at the mouth of the Ammonoosuc today. There are dams on the Connecticut River as well, 3 miles and 8 miles above Woodsville, at Ryegate and Monroe, so when I resumed my northward journey on July 8, I decided to travel by bicycle instead of canoe. I parked the car near the old depot — Woodsville used to be something of a railroad town before steam locomotives and passenger trains disappeared — and began pedaling along the east bank of the Connecticut at a spot called the Narrows.

The valley opened up a bit, and the highway veered away from the river. It was cool for July, but the corn was waist-high and black-eyed Susans brightened the shoulders of the road, which went up and down, climbing over low rises and dipping into hollows, from open fields to woods, from sunshine into deep shade and back into the light. A shiny brown UPS truck went by in the opposite direction, and I overtook a slow tractor; otherwise there was no traffic. It was all over on the Vermont side of the valley. The river stayed out of sight, but I didn't need to see it. As I rode along I found that I could imagine the river perfectly: the minnows darting under the canoe, the pressure of the current against the blade of the paddle, the fresh lilt of the riffles, the cobbled texture of gravel against the butt of the setting pole, the swallows skimming over the water. In a way, it was more vivid for *not* being able to see it.

I passed through the little village of Monroe, the site of a diminutive, 13-megawatt NEPCO dam, and continued until I came to a fork in the road 3 miles later where the left branch went down a hill to cross a bridge to the village of Barnet, Vermont. The little sternwheeler *Barnet*, which made the first steam-powered ascent of Enfield Rapids in 1842, was named after the town, but it never came within a hundred miles of it because the boat proved too wide to fit through the locks at Bellows Falls. Another steamboat called *Vermont* made it past Bellows Falls but was stopped by the narrow canal at Sumner Falls.

In 1831, the tiny steamboat *John Ledyard* passed through the Sumner Falls Canal and the Wilder Canal but ran hard aground in the riffles below Woodsville. Barnet remained out of reach.

About a mile north of Barnet village the railroad, U.S. 5, and I-91 all take their final leave of the valley, forsaking the master stream to follow the tributary Passumpsic River up through St. Johnsbury and Lyndonville, Vermont, to the height of land at Burke and on to the Canadian border. I stuck with the Connecticut, on the New Hampshire side, and the road began to climb an intimidating hill. It leveled off and then climbed again, not so steeply now, but with no end in sight. I was churning away in the lowest of my twelve gears, sweat running into my eyes and forming salty drops on the tip of my nose. A pickup truck whooshed by in a blast of warm, exhaust-flavored air, and the driver looked at me, frowning, as if to say "You dumb son of a bitch." I could certainly see why the railroad hadn't been built there. The valley had narrowed to a steep, V-shaped gash. In fact, the river drops 18 feet to the mile for the next 20 miles, a radical departure from the normal gradient of 6 to 10 inches per mile. The course, moreover, cuts across the grain of the mountains in a northeasterly direction (as you travel upstream), and this caused successive glaciers to drop massive amounts of debris and boulders into the riverbed, the result being rapids, more than 20 miles of boiling whitewater known as Fifteen Mile Falls. No less an engineer than DeWitt Clinton, the builder of the Erie Canal, examined this stretch of river and declared that it would never be opened to navigation.

The road went up and up with an occasional dip, and then climbed some more until it leveled out on the crest of a ridge. Cleared fields afforded a 60-mile view across the valley and deep into Vermont. I went under a buzzing power line suspended from spidery steel towers and turned left on the road to Comerford Dam, coasting downgrade through cornfields and then woods to the shore of the pond.

Comerford is a colossal structure, a dam you might expect to find plugging some great canyon in Arizona. Although the Connecticut's flow here is only about half what it is at Bellows Falls, Comerford's gross head of 179 feet more than compensates for that. The generators have a capacity of 168 magawatts (versus 50 megawatts at Bellows Falls). Herbert Hoover flicked the switch that put Comerford on-line in 1930. It was the largest conventional hydroelectric facility in New England at the time, but it has since been surpassed by Moore Dam, 8 miles upstream. Together they have a capacity of 367 megawatts.

Hydroplane races are held on the Moore Pond, and you have to wonder what the old rivermen would think of that. Fifteen Mile Falls were the most dangerous rapids on the log drives, and more than one riverman drowned here. It is impossible to say exactly how difficult the rapids actually were, since the rivermen did not have the uniform rating system that recreational canoeists do now, but surely this was one of the finest and longest pieces of big river whitewater in the eastern United States. Muliken's Pitch, the steepest drop, was right where Comerford Dam stands today. It is said that when the dam was being built, the workers dug up a number of old pork barrels with caulked boots still inside. A pork barrel was the only coffin for some rivermen.

12 ❧ BARNET

to LANCASTER

North Country

*T*HE HILL COUNTRY of northern New England pleases all the senses, makes a man feel old and wise. It seems strange that such a rumpled topography should soothe the mind, but undeniably it does.

It is always fresh and breezy up on the ridgetops — a good 10 or 15 degrees cooler than down in the valley on a steamy July afternoon — although you pay for that summer comfort, of course, when the blizzards of January come raging down from Canada. Still, this is a beautiful land. Men have been wresting a living from its thin, rocky soil, against all odds, with varying degrees of success, with stubbornness and ingenuity, for more than a century and a half.

In May of 1982, I was driving from Montpelier, Vermont, to St. Johnsbury on a day when the trees at the higher elevations were just beginning to leaf. The car had crested a rise and swung around a curve when a horse-drawn manure spreader trundled across the road. Was it worth a picture? I pulled off

onto the shoulder, and when the spreader came back for another load the man driving the horses told me to go up in the
pasture where I might get a better shot.

He was right. Mount Mansfield stood off to the west, the
ski trails still covered with snow near the summit. To the east
the land fell away in green ridges, then rose up again in powerful, swelling waves to the frothy white mass of Mount Washington and the Presidential Range. As near as I could tell, the
pasture straddled a height of land that divides a tributary of the
Winooski (which flows into Lake Champlain) and a tributary of
the Passumpsic (which flows into the Connecticut at Barnet).

This fellow's house sat in a slight hollow directly across the
road from a weatherbeaten barn he later told me was built in
1794. Through an open door I could see cows flicking their tails.
Several brand-new sleds of the type used by horse loggers sat
out front, lined up in a neat row to catch the eye of prospective
customers. A big yellow Michigan bucket loader was parked by
the manure pile. There was a fair-sized sawmill, too, with logs
and finished lumber piled around it.

I watched the spreader go back and forth across the field
for a while, then the driver let the horses rest. He was a short,
stocky man about fifty-five years old, with a round, wrinkled
brown face like a walnut shell. He reached into the pocket of his
canvas coat for a foil pouch of Days Work chewing tobacco.

"This here is Celeste," he said. "She's pure-bred Belgian
mare. This other one is just plain horse."

Celeste's long black mane was streaked with silver. I asked
the man if he used the horses much, and he said no. "We don't
have the time for it anymore, what with the sawmill and all that.
But I guess I'll keep horses until I die. They're good in the
woods, you know. Nothing better. I've got one boy back up
there today. He says there's three foot of snow on the ground."

Another son was spreading manure with a tractor. I had
counted at least five old tractors on the place, along with a good
bit of other machinery, including snowmobiles, hay balers, piles

of wheel rims, gears, sprockets, flywheels, engine blocks, and the like. It takes a lot of spare parts to keep a sawmill running.

"We put the horses on the stone boat," the man said, "when we dug the cellar for the new house. The old place like to fell down two years ago, and I had to do something. Some mornings it'd be down near zero in the kitchen when I got out of bed."

"Look," he said, "it's almost coffee-break time. Come down to the house and I'll show it to you."

The front room still smelled faintly of sawn lumber. A giant wood-burning range with bright metal fittings sat in the middle of the floor. A pan of hot peach cobbler, coffee cups, and a big metal pitcher of milk were set out on the table. A little later we went to see the cellar.

"They wanted thirty-five hundred dollars to pour concrete," the man said. "I couldn't see that, so I got these granite scraps from down to Barre. This right here is Venezuelan granite. This pinkish stone is from Québec. There's some African granite in here, too."

A big flat slab of polished stone the size of a pool table had been set into one corner of the cellar to serve as a workbench. I began to wonder if there was anything this man couldn't do. He was a stonemason, a sawyer, a carpenter, a dairyman, a teamster, a blacksmith — all the doors in the house had handmade wrought-iron hinges — and a first-rate mechanic. He was a master free-lance technologist.

"I guess I never really worked for anyone else in my life," he said. On the other hand, he benefited from the same government subsidies that go to all dairy farmers, and I had noticed the blue and white Agri-Mark* sign on the barn. He took advantage of whatever worked.

---

*Agri-Mark is a four-thousand-member dairy cooperative with cheese factories as far away as Utah and a citrus plant in Florida.

I got back in the car and continued on to St. Johnsbury, cruising along ridgetops at first, then dropping way down into the deep valley of the Passumpsic River, finally crossing I-91 on the outskirts of town. This was the last section of I-91 to be completed (in 1978), and now I-93 was under construction. I drove out to take a look at it.

Instead of following the natural features of the landscape, I-93 slices across the grain of the mountains. The road cuts are stupendous. When the engineers came to a cliff, they didn't go around it; they blew it up. I stood in the afternoon sun for a while and watched snorting herds of huge lime green earth-moving machines rumble back and forth, their low-slung bellies heavy with crushed rock. The air was hot with dust and fumes, and presently my eye was attracted to bright plastic ribbons fluttering from survey stakes in a swath of newly cleared forest. There was precision at work here as well as brute force; gradient and curvature had been calculated to the fraction of an inch. Americans are very good at building highways, and I-93 seemed to be a virtuoso performance. Yet it wasn't as impressive as I had expected. What, after all, was this little scratch in the dirt compared to the great trenches, cirques, and ravines gouged out by Ice Age glaciers? Or, for that matter, to the billions upon billions of tons of material removed by running water?

❧

The Vermont portion of I-93, from St. Johnsbury to the Connecticut River just below Moore Dam, was finished in the fall of 1982, and I made my first trip over the highway in July 1983. It was a chilly day, with a glowering stormy sky and a strong wind that threatened to lift the canoe right off the top of the car. Any desire I had to explore the 3,490-acre Moore Pond vanished at the sight of the whitecaps and the streaks of foam blowing across the steely gray surface of the water. I headed up the New Hampshire side of the valley slowly, crawling along behind a logging truck, passing through the little hamlet of Dalton, and finally came to a dirt pullout by the mouth of the Johns River. Gilman, Vermont — a small village built around a big Georgia Pacific paper mill — was about 3 miles downstream on the Connecticut. The Fifteen Mile Falls rapids began at Gilman, but the paper company dam eliminated the uppermost section of whitewater.

I was more worried about the wind than the current, and I sat in the car for a while with the heater going, trying to decide if it was worth the trouble. In my time on the river, I have come to dislike a headwind above all other adversities. A current you can deal with. You can take it as a challenge, and there is satisfaction in overcoming it. A wind is simply a nuisance. It witches around, hitting you first on one side and then the other, gusting and dying off. You can't see it. You can't predict what it's going to do. It's infuriating. A canoe is exquisitely responsive to the paddle on still water, but in a bad wind you are virtually helpless. On a big lake, where the wind has room to kick up waves, it can keep you on the beach for days.

Once I finally gathered up the motivation to put the canoe in the river, most of my energy went into holding a straight course. If I stopped paddling for a few seconds, the wind drove me backward. I could hardly move forward at all, so I was reduced to using the motor. It was either that or quit. I learned later that right about that time, the weather observatory on the summit of Mount Washington was recording gusts of 95 miles an hour. Here in the valley, the wind was strong enough to strip leaves off the trees. A sudden blast caught me by surprise and started to push the bow around. Once it began to swing I couldn't stop it, even with the motor running flat out, and I ended up facing downstream. A half-hour later, however, there was almost no wind at all. I can't explain it. Swallows came out to feed, and kingfishers chattered agitatedly. A great blue heron worked the shallows along the bank. He took off as I came closer, unfolding those big wings and lurching wearily into the air, only to land a hundred yards upstream — until I put him up again and the entire performance was repeated. Apparently this was going to go on for some time. The heron seemed determined to stay one jump ahead of the canoe.

I passed under a covered bridge. The roof, the roadway, and part of the walls had been removed, exposing wooden truss members. (The purpose of the roof and walls is to keep the load-bearing truss assembly out of the weather.) Repair work would resume on Monday morning. The river curved around to the right until the canoe was pointing due east, now with a wide floodplain rolling back from either bank. This part of the valley was once known as the Upper Coos and the name lives on — at least on the New Hampshire side — in Coos County, which includes the entire northern tip of the state. Berlin, New Hampshire, a paper mill town on the Androscoggin River, is the metropolis of Coos County, with Lancaster, Groveton, and Colebrook the principal towns on the Connecticut River. Lancaster is the farthest south and the largest, with a population of about 4,000. There are no large towns on the Vermont side, which explains why many of the Vermonters in these parts were actually born in New Hampshire, since that's where the hospitals are. The landscape is as green in the summer as it is anywhere else, but there are always reminders of the severe climate. Spruce and fir grow thick on open hillsides, not just in shady ravines or on mountaintops. There is no cottonwood, few oak, and even poison ivy is scarce. In the spring, the wildflowers bloom a week later than they do just 30 miles downstream (where riverside elevations are almost 500 feet lower), and the maple leaves change a week or two earlier in the fall. Winters are best left to the imagination. The year-round, *average* temperature in Pittsburg, New Hampshire, near the Connecticut Lakes, is 37 degrees. There were still a few caribou in these woods as recently as 1910.

Presently I came to some piles of stone, like crude bridge piers, in the middle of the river, held in place by heavy log cribbing. Piers such as these are a common sight in the north country; they were used to anchor booms that held back the log drives. Several lumber companies usually had drives on the river at the same time, and the booms kept the logs from mixing. It was still cold, and the blue heron was still ahead of me, after 4 miles, as the Connecticut meandered across its floodplain between high banks. On the New Hampshire side, however, there was a break where cattle had been coming down to drink, and I used it to land the canoe. I climbed up the muddy slope and found an ancient, immobilized Chevrolet flatbed truck. It might have been red once, but it was purple now, soft and subtle, with a warm undertone of rust. You could mix paint for hours and not match that shade. Fifty or sixty Holstein cows grazed nearby, all facing the same direction. Off in the distance a big white farmhouse stood in the field, like a grounded iceberg, with the tall, dark blue peaks of the Pilot Range rising beyond, their tops sliced off by somber clouds. Rain squalls walked across lower hills to the west.

Something about the truck touched me. The glass in the old-fashioned divided windshield — the kind that cranks open to let in a breeze — was cracked in a star pattern by a single bullethole in each pane. The wheels were sunk to the hubs in the pasture sod, and moss grew thick on the rotting planks of the bed. The truck was slowly returning to the elements. I squatted to read the lettering still faintly visible on the cab door:

J. J. VIETTE
CONTRACTOR
LITTLETON, N.H.
call 322

I got back in the canoe, and a short piece later the river made a sharp turn to the right, to a northeasterly heading. It held that course for a mile, then doubled back on itself in a tight 180-degree kink before beginning a broad curve in the opposite direction, like this:

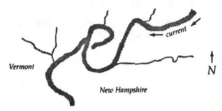

The land enclosed by the cut off oxbow lake is part of New Hampshire even though it is on the Vermont side of the river. Such are the hazards of using an alluvial waterway for a state line. .

I stopped to pick raspberries, taking only those I could reach from the canoe without standing up. There were plenty of them, ripe to the point of dropping off the vine, so sweet and soft they melted when you pressed them against the roof of your mouth. The wind was completely calm and the mosquitoes were out, cold or no cold. The river continued to go around bends, the bottom gradually changing from silt to sand as the current became lively. Having no map, I wasn't too sure just where I was until the mouth of the Israel River appeared on the right, partially hidden behind an island. Two muskrats plopped into the water, and while I waited for them to surface, the canoe passed directly over an old wooden wagon wheel. Then I spotted another wheel on the bottom, the metal tire almost completely rusted away. The river was shallow here; could this have once been a ford? Probably not. More likely someone had junked a wagon. You know the old Yankee saying: use it up, wear it out, make it do, or do without — then throw it in the river. White men have been tossing their junk in the Connecticut River for three hundred and fifty years, although I suppose this wagon could have washed away in a flood.

Barnet to Lancaster

The Israel River seemed like a good place to turn the canoe around and head back downstream. The great blue heron that had stayed ahead of me all this way was now standing on a gravel bar, poised for flight. Ten minutes later, when I took a final look over my shoulder, he was still there.

13 🦫 LANCASTER

to NORTH STRATFORD

The Big Woods

I DIDN'T REALIZE that cows had such bony behinds," Sue Weingarten said to me.

"Look at all those killdeer," I said. The killdeer, twenty-five or thirty of them, were skittering around between the cows' legs, calling back and forth, on a sandy beach beside the Connecticut, deep in the Upper Coos, north of Groveton, New Hampshire. Killdeer are more often seen in pairs. Even so, I might not have given this flock a second glance if I hadn't already seen, just a half-hour earlier, a mob of red-winged blackbirds massed in some bushes on the riverbank. Could these birds conceivably be getting ready to migrate? I couldn't believe it. Not on the twenty-eighth of July. I didn't even want to think about the short northern summer coming to an end.

And of course it wasn't. Not yet. I had been keeping track of several merganser families, and the ducklings were still tiny. They wouldn't be ready to fly for weeks. Just the day before, when Susie and I took the canoe out for a spin on Maidstone Lake, we saw a pair of loons (one of the twelve nesting pairs counted in Vermont that year) with two fuzzy gray chicks. The chicks were a good size, it is true, but their flight feathers weren't even starting to come in. Summer wasn't over. Killdeer and blackbirds aside, the afternoon of the twenty-eighth turned out to be a classic July dog day, with the temperature up in the nineties, Queen Anne's lace in the fields, and steamy humidity followed by heat lightning in the evening. The rain held off until the middle of the night, or at least that's when I was first aware of the drops pattering on the tent.

It was still raining in the morning, and I didn't have the heart to fool with a fire, so we drove down to a diner near the paper mill in Groveton. Big logging trucks were parked five deep outside, and Susie, who teaches high school French, pointed out grammatical errors in the bilingual menu. It looked as though it was going to rain all day, so we decided to go up and take a look at the Nulhegan River.

The Nulhegan is a treat in any weather. It is almost unique among the Connecticut's tributaries because it, and all of its branches, are completely free-flowing. In fact, it is the largest free-flowing watershed in the Connecticut drainage system. It is also relatively wild, taversed by just one paved highway and the Canadian National Railway, although the woods are marred by clear cuts. Paper companies own most of the land. The 230-square-mile watershed includes all or parts of the towns of Bloomfield, Ferdinand, Brighton, Avery's Gore, and Lewis, Vermont, the latter two having no public road, post office, zip code, or permanent population. Logging is the major business, as it is throughout the northernmost Connecticut River watershed.

Along with running water, wood has been an important natural resource in New England since the beginning of white settlement. Shipbuilding provided the first large market for Yankee timber, and the eighteenth century was America's wooden age, with wood being used for everything from broomsticks to potash to scientific instruments. Large-scale logging, in which lumber companies owned vast tracts of wilderness, did not begin until the 1800s, first in Maine and then elsewhere. The Connecticut Valley Lumber Company (CVLC) dominated logging operations in northeastern Vermont and in the Connecticut Lakes region of New Hampshire; George Van Dyke, a quintessential, cigar-smoking timber baron, dominated the CVLC. He was born poor in rural Québec, never married, and remained devoted to his mother throughout his life; when it came to business, he let nothing interfere with expediency, often using physical intimidation to get his way. Van Dyke went on his first log drive at the age of fourteen, and it was as a riverman that he made his reputation.

A drivable stream was the first requirement for a logging operation in the north woods. If a stream of sufficient width and depth did not exist, the timber wasn't cut. Because a river like the Nulhegan, or the upper Connecticut for that matter, only had enough water to float logs for a month or two in the spring, the loggers worked accordingly. Summer was quiet, with time for cruising the woods and selecting the stands to be cut. In the fall the camps were spruced up. Hay and feed were brought in for the horses — logging used a lot of horsepower — and work began on the tote roads. The river itself received attention too. Snags and stumps were removed from the bed, and the small dams that were used to control the flow and increase the depth of the water were repaired. The main crew arrived after the first snowfall, and trees were felled all winter long. By March or April, the riverside landings were piled high with logs. The drive began as soon as the ice went out.

The spring thaw on a north woods river is not a gentle event. When the ice goes out it tends to go all at once, in a great chaotic rush. The raging current, swollen with snowmelt and heavy rains, is easily capable of tossing multiton blocks of ice up on the banks like pieces of cork. The rapids roar and smoke, and good-sized boulders tremble. It strains the far limits of credibility to think that men actually rode logs in these conditions, but ride them they did, jumping nimbly from log to log and working frantically to prevent jams. A certain amount of jamming, however, was inevitable, and picking jams apart was the most dangerous part of the drive. Dynamite was used as a last resort, but a jam could usually be cleared by removing or loosening a few key logs that were holding the others back. Then the crew had to scramble out of the way in a big hurry. Anyone who wasn't quick enough stood to be crushed, maimed, or knocked unconscious and drowned.

If the life of the riverman was not particularly safe, then neither was it comfortable. Riding a log might be glamorous, and undoubtedly exhilarating, but spills were common. Even if a man didn't slip, he was in the water a lot anyway, wading in the frigid current to heave and pry on misbehaving logs. In fact, the rivermen were in the water more often than out of it. They worked wet and they slept wet, rolled up in soggy blankets.

Boats had only a limited utility on small streams like the Nulhegan but were mandatory on larger rivers. The standard boat of the log drives was an admirable craft called a batteau that looked something like a Grand Banks fishing dory. It could be rowed or poled and had great stability in whitewater. Whole fleets of batteaus accompanied the Connecticut River log drive — one of the longest log drives in the country — which went all the way from the Connecticut Lakes to the mills at Mount Tom and Holyoke. It took about five hundred men to work the drive down through Fifteen Mile Falls, about half that number on the broader, smoother waters below. A train of seven or eight horse-drawn wagons called the wangan followed the drive along the banks. The cook and his helpers dished up four big meals a day. Below Woodsville the wangan was put on a raft, as were the horses used to pull logs off the banks.

Entire towns turned out to watch the logs go by, but the drive sometimes provided trouble along with entertainment. When the logs jammed up against the piers of a bridge, the entire span might be carried away. Jams also caused local flooding, and farmers complained about logs stranded in riverside fields. Mills were inconvenienced by logs too, having to shut down turbines and waterwheels as the drive approached. The drive could pass small dams without great difficulty, but the larger hydroelectric dams that were just beginning to appear in the early part of the twentieth century were another matter. The first of the present NEPCO dams, however, was not finished until the 1920s, and the last drive of long logs on the Connecticut took place in 1915. Smaller pulpwood drives were still using the upper Connecticut until the mid-1940s, and the last log drive in the United States, on the Kennebec River in Maine, was in 1976.

✺

The old-time rivermen were on my mind as Susie and I drove along the lower Nulhegan, but there wasn't enough water in the rapids to float a canoe, much less a log drive. A little farther upstream, however, the terrain flattened out, and the river meandered placidly through woods and alder swamps. The rain had let up for the time being, and I found a good put-in spot by a bridge near a large boggy area that spread out toward mountains in the west. I slid the canoe down the bank and we shoved off downstream.

The dense, dripping spruce closed in around us, and after a hundred yards it felt as though we were in the midst of a trackless wilderness. The silky current flowed along in absolute silence. Dangling mats of sphagnum moss hung over the banks on the outside of the curves where the river undercut the forest floor, toppling trees. As is true of most north woods streams, the water in the Nulhegan was stained brown but was still clear and cold, like strong iced tea.

I killed a deerfly, taking the time to crunch it between thumb and forefinger. It made such a gratifying sound — a rich crackle — that I killed two more. There is usually a good supply of biting insects up here. Drifting on downstream, we went around a bend in time to see a great horned owl take off from a dead tree. I hooted a couple of times and the big bird circled back, then vanished. Damselflies with glossy black wings and slender, bright turquoise abdomens skimmed over the water. Small trout hung in the deep, clear pools. There were well-worn game trails leading into the alder thickets and fresh moose tracks on the bars. The entire Nulhegan drainage area is pretty damp, and it can be hard to say, sometimes, just where the bogs leave off and the forest begins. "Letting daylight into the swamp" was the phrase commonly used by loggers when they moved into a new stand of timber up here.

At first the lumber companies wanted only the old-growth white pine, and when they were gone, the prime spruce sawtimber. There was no market for spruce and fir pulpwood until about 1880; hardwood wasn't touched at all, because the logs wouldn't float. Then railroads began to appear in the woods. A few logging railroads, such as the one on the East Branch of the Nulhegan, were built specifically to get at large hardwood stands, while other railroads sprung up out of a desire to exploit the remaining stocks of virgin spruce and pine in the high valleys, mainly in the White Mountains, where the terrain was too steep for river driving.

Logging railroads were temporary affairs but expensive nonetheless, and once a company had committed funds to building a railroad, it felt obliged to get its money's worth out of it as quickly as possible. All the best timber was cut, along with much that was worthless, since trees left standing on hillsides interfered with rolling logs down to the landings at the railhead. Slash from these clear cuts was left behind, and when it dried it ignited mammoth forest fires, denuding thousands of acres. The valley of the Zealand River, a headwaters tributary of the Ammonoosuc, is a prime example. Until 1881, the Zealand drainage area was pristine wilderness; scarcely a decade later it had become a smoldering wasteland.

The Zealand Valley Railroad, which ran from 1884 to 1897, was the first railroad venture of one J. E. Henry, otherwise known as "the Grand Duke of Lincoln." Vintage photographs show a skinny old goat with close-cropped white hair and a gleam in his eye. Like George Van Dyke, J.E. was born into backwoods poverty and died a millionaire several times over. Henry, however, got his start as a teamster, which perhaps explains his attraction to the iron horse. After the Zealand Valley debacle, he moved on to the Pemigewasset country where he built his masterpiece, the East Branch & Lincoln. It became the largest and lasted the longest of the seventeen logging railroads in the White Mountains.

One thing that can be said for J. E. Henry and his fellow lumber barons is that they never tried to gloss over what they were doing. They were cutting timber to make a profit, and within the blinkered scope of this ambition they brought stunning energy, determination, and will power to the task at hand, which was considerable, given the primitive technology available. Henry was a shrewd manipulator of woodsmen, machinery, horses, and money, and it is hard not to admire him for it. It is also probably fair to say that Henry, by virtue of the swath he cut across the White Mountains, did as much to shock the general public into environmental awareness as any New Englander before or since. One result was the passage of the Weeks Act in 1911, which authorized the federal government to purchase private timberland and which led to the creation of the White Mountain National Forest.

J.E.'s East Branch & Lincoln continued to haul logs until the

1940s, long after the Grand Duke was dead and buried. Work on a logging railroad up the East Branch of the Nulhegan River did not begin until 1920, and by that time the logging industry was changing. In a significant departure from earlier practice, the CVLC leased the Nulhegan hardwood stumpage to an outside firm, the Warner Sugar Refining Company, rather than do the cutting itself. The sugar company built the railroad, ran the woods camps, erected a large stave and heading mill in North Stratford, New Hampshire, and began to manufacture sugar barrels.

But the demand for wooden barrels disappeared within a few years, as paper containers took over the market. In fact, the pulpwood cut had already surpassed the sawlog cut in northern New England. In the short term, this was bad for the forest because pulp could be made from smaller trees, including the previously ignored balsam fir, and it was definitely bad for the rivers because pulp mills were massive polluters. On the other hand, a pulp mill was a major industrial installation, taking years to earn back the company's investment, and this forced the owners to think about assuring a supply of wood for the future. The 1920s thus saw the beginning of modern industrial forestry.

Another new development of the 1920s was the Lombard log hauler, a steam-powered device that looked like a small steam locomotive but ran on treads instead of steel rails. Later versions of the Lombard used a gasoline engine, foreshadowing the eventual supremacy of the diesel logging truck. In the meantime, the Nulhegan woods were pretty much played out. The sugar barrel railroad was pulled up in 1927, and the CVLC sold most of its land in northern New Hampshire and Vermont to the St. Regis Paper Company. Intensive logging resumed in the Nulhegan drainage in 1964, and, indeed, I could hear chain saws off in the distance as we floated along in the canoe. Now that log drives are a thing of the past, about the only time that the woods are quiet is during mud season, when the ground is too soft for skidders to work and the private logging roads are in danger of washing out.

❧

A silvery mist hung in the air the next morning when we put the canoe in the Connecticut River at Stratford, New Hampshire. The river was as clear as a mountain brook, and as we paddled upstream I leaned over the gunwale to watch small clouds of sand being blown along the bottom by the current. The grains moved in a definite pattern, accelerating here, accumulating there. This, I said to Susie, is how bars form. Hydrologists, of course, have studied the process — and everything else about a river's behavior — in great detail. I have a hydrology text entitled *Rivers: Form and Process in Alluvial Channels*. Although just a paperback edition of 358 pages, it sits heavy in your hands, and the dense prose, liberally studded with equations and formulae, bears down like a mudslide, overwhelming you with turbid discussions of noncohesive grains, submerged particle weights, turning movements, fluid drag forces, downstream fulcrums, and packing coefficients. It is beyond my power to understand very much of this, but it is enough to know that someone does, that the river is a great rush of mathematics, a relentless flow of unbreakable laws, exquisite tensions, minute balances. It is perfect in its form, always, and utterly inanimate, without the slightest speck of intelligence or awareness to direct its infinite complexity. Perhaps, however, the complexity itself is something like a soul. The brain goes numb attempting to decipher it, but the body somehow understands, the way a trout or a muskrat understands. The tension of the current is transmitted through the blade of the paddle, through the hull of the canoe, and the flow becomes a part of you.

Every canoeist, if he spends much time on the river, becomes a lay hydrologist, a practical student of moving water, and if he uses the setting pole he takes an interest in the form of the riverbed as well. What is the bottom like? Is it bedrock, gravel, sand, silt, or mud? Is the gravel loose or packed? Is there a growth of weed? Is there algae on the rocks? How do these things correlate to the flow and to the landscape? This section of the Connecticut, in the Upper Coos, is an excellent field laboratory for the casual study of sine-generated meandering curves, cut banks, oxbow lakes, and the riffle-pool sequence. I quickly discovered that Leopold and Langbein are right — the riffles *do* alternate from one side to the other — and I put the information to use to avoid having to get out and drag the canoe over shallow bars. The river attempts to minimize energy loss, and the alert canoeist will do the same.

There used to be two dams on this part of the river, one about 15 miles upstream from Stratford at Lyman Falls, the other about 20 miles downstream at Guildhall, Vermont, but both have washed out, and the Connecticut is now essentially free-flowing all the way from Beecher Falls to the head of Gilman Pond. It is gratifying to find rapids where there used to be deadwater. The average flow in this vicinity is about 1,550 cubic feet per second, not much greater than that of the White River. The Connecticut has become a little stream in a big valley. U.S. 3 runs along the New Hampshire side, but because the river meanders so much, the road seldom comes close to the water. Occasionally Susie and I saw a house or a barn, or heard someone out on a tractor, mowing hay. Otherwise it was quiet. About two o'clock the mist began to burn off, and we passed the handsome granite piers of a long-abandoned Maine Central Railroad bridge. The thought occurred to me (not for the first time) that stone bridge piers may someday be among the last manmade objects standing in New England.

Or perhaps not. It doesn't matter. The life of a bridge pier, or anything else made by man, is of small moment in the ancient history of this river valley, which wears its age well — in the gentle but still proud contours of the mountains, in the generous breadth of the floodplain, in the round bottom stones of the riverbed, perfect as eggs. The river does good work. The plates came together, the crust buckled, and this is what running water produced: this green masterpiece. Yet the river hardly seems equal to the task, at least not now, in the summer, as it swishes transparently over the bars, barely murmuring, changing colors, shimmering, sparkling, swift and exquisite, draining through your fingers when you dip a cupped hand over the gunwale, leaving the skin cool afterward, like a faded memory. Running water is the essence of impermanence. But it will still be flowing when even these hills are gone. A river possesses a good, practical kind of immortality.

The mouth of Paul Stream appeared on the left after a couple of miles, and that was far enough. The sun had begun to heat things up, making the afternoon perfect for a lazy downstream float. Monumental white cumulus clouds drifted slowly above the green hills, but nothing else seemed to move except the flowing water. Susie switched ends with me, and I sat in the bow, watching the shadow of the canoe slide silently and precisely along the sandy riverbed.

I stayed up late that night, drinking beer from a warm six-pack that I found in the back of the car and putting logs on the fire, mesmerized by sparks rising into a cold black sky full of stars. The loons started in sometime past midnight, calling back and forth across Maidstone Lake, wailing and laughing in high, clear, unearthly voices that echoed off the mountains, just as loons have been doing in the north woods these past 60 million years.

14 ❧ NORTH STRATFORD

to PITTSBURG

Canot du nord

AUGUST 11. I returned to the Nulhegan River and put the canoe in at the same spot where Susie and I had launched it before, heading upstream this time. The river was no wider than a brook at that point, and I had little hope of going very far. After a couple hundred yards of shallow, noisy riffles I came to the first obstacle, a brand-new beaver dam. A beaver was sitting on it, watching me intently. He slipped into the water as I came closer without so much as a single tail slap, and that was the last I saw of him.

Above the dam the river smoothed out and began to meander, passing through a spruce wood and into an extensive swampy area of alder thickets, ripe blueberries, open marsh, and clumps of larches. The water in the deep pools, which normally appears clear and brown, had become dark red in the sunlight. Specks of mica glittered on the sandy bottom. Yellow warblers darted around in the underbrush. Suddenly a tremendous, explosive thrashing erupted in a dense mass of alders by the bank, and I whirled around to see a cow moose rise to her feet and go storming off in a great panic. Actually, I saw parts of the moose — a length of leg, a hump of shoulder, patches of brown hide — but there was no mistaking the noise. Only a moose could make such a commotion. The huge animal crashed through the thickets like an overloaded logging truck hitting potholes. I got out of the canoe to look for tracks and found the mashed-down spot where the moose must have been sleeping.

The river showed no signs of petering out. It followed a whimsical course, curving and looping and doubling back on itself, with numerous false channels leading to dead ends. After several miles of this I came to a logging road bridge and then the Canadian National Railway at a place called Wenlock Siding. In the old days, there used to be a sawmill here — it cut ties for the East Branch sugar barrel railroad — and as recently as the winter of 1982–1983 the spot was used as a St. Regis log storage and loading area. The mobile slasher, a huge blue machine that can convert a bundle of tree-size logs into 4-foot lengths of pulp in the blink of an eye, sat idle now, the great circular blade brown with rust.

The sky had begun to cloud over, becoming ominous, and the distant mountains, when they were visible through breaks in the trees, had turned from green to blue. The river continued to twine around curves, and it seemed to be getting deeper. The Nulhegan is a stream that breaks the rules, becoming less steep as you approach its source. The long profile looks something like this:

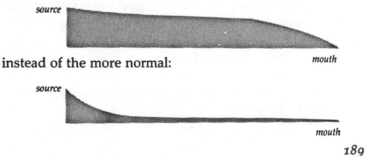

source

mouth

instead of the more normal:

source

mouth

North Stratford to Pittsburg

The lower Nulhegan tumbles down rapids that are too bony to run in August, but the upper half of the river, which meanders across a broad, bowl-like basin, will float a canoe all summer long. The deepest parts of the river, however, are also the narrowest, and the alders on the banks reach out to interlace their branches above the water, forming a leafy tunnel. You have to bash your way through these thickets, often by stretching out in the bottom of the canoe and pulling yourself along hand over hand, grasping the branches. Every time I thought about quitting, more open water appeared ahead.

The noise of the breaking branches alerted the beavers and muskrats; I could hear them plopping into the river as I went around the blind curves. There were low beaver dams every half-mile or so, and they could be crossed without difficulty, usually without my having to get out of the canoe. At one point a glossy black damselfly lighted on the center thwart and rode along with me for a while, and a bit later a monarch butterfly appeared, a sure sign that autumn was not very far off. Indeed, it was getting colder and rain was beginning to fall, gently at first, bringing out dozens of tiny, fluttering white moths. Delicate round bubbles drifted down the dark river. I managed to stay fairly dry except for the gap between the bottom of my slicker and the tops of my hip boots. Also, a cold trickle of water found its way into my sleeve each time I raised my right arm to plant the setting pole on the bottom.

I turned around about three o'clock, and the current, which I had barely noticed coming upstream, moved the canoe at a good speed. The Nulhegan flowed smoothly and silently in what had become a steady, soaking rain, and thick wreaths of fog settled about the shoulders of the mountains. The wet alder leaves took on a dull sheen in the dim gray light; even the warblers and the cedar waxwings seemed to be subdued. Knowing that I would sleep indoors was a great comfort; it made the rain feel cool and soothing.

August 12. It was bitter cold in the morning, with a leaden sky that looked like snow. I launched the canoe at the inlet creek of Nulhegan Pond and drifted downstream through lily pads, scattering lethargic frogs. There is always a chance of surprising a moose on such a pond at this time of year, but all I did was put up a duck. Nulhegan Pond appears to be very deep. It was probably gouged out by the glacier. The water was black and choppy. Marsh grass and feathery larches ringed the shoreline, and dark spruce woods stretched off toward the mountains. I turned up my collar against the wind.

The pond is not quite at the headwaters of the Nulhegan River. The actual height of land, about a mile up the inlet creek, is a barely perceptible hump. A short, level portage takes you first to Spectacle Pond, then to Island Pond, both of which drain into Lake Memphremagog and ultimately into the St. Lawrence River. There is no easier carry across the Connecticut–St. Lawrence divide. The surrounding mountains, which are actually a northwestern extension of the White Mountains, are relatively low and stand well apart from one another, making the topography of the region (if not the climate) fairly gentle. It is classic canoe country, much like Maine or northern Minnesota or the vast north woods of Canada.

In Labrador, Québec, and Ontario, in northern Manitoba, Saskatchewan, and Alberta, from the Atlantic to the Rockies to the Arctic tundra, the northern boreal forest predominates. Like the Nulhegan woods, it is flat or rolling terrain, cold and lonely, much of it underlaid by the ancient rock of the Canadian Shield. It is everywhere splattered with lakes — at least a hundred thousand in Saskatchewan alone — and veined with rushing rivers. One third of the fresh water on the planet is in Canada. This is the native habitat of the bark canoe, and though the Indians provided the genius and the forest the materials, it was the reality of long-distance travel in the north woods — shallow streams, rapids, stormy lakes, and frequent portages — that shaped the canoe's design.

With a canoe, a hunter could follow game wherever he chose, and thus the canoe made the fur trade possible. Beaver was the great prize. Its fur was made into felt and felt into beaver hats, which became popular in Paris and London, allowing Canada's first major industry to be founded on a whim of European fashion. Bark canoes provided the indispensable link between Montréal and the remote trading posts. Indians did the trapping, Englishmen made the financial arrangements, and French-Canadian voyageurs brought the beaver pelts back to civilization.

The voyageurs were hired hands, employed by the big companies that came to dominate the fur trade. Gigantic thirty-man canoes (the *canot du maître*) were used on the first stage of the voyageurs' outward journey in the spring, from Montréal to Grand Portage, on the northwest shore of Lake Superior; the smaller *canot du nord* was used on the second stage, which took the voyageurs deep into the wilderness. Because of the great distances involved (as much as 4,000 miles a round trip) and the shortness of the northern summer, there was no time to be wasted. The voyageurs rose in the dark, paddled two or three hours before breakfast, then paddled straight through the day until nightfall. The canoe itself, however, was treated with the utmost care, since the bark hull was fragile. It was never rammed up on a beach for loading or unloading, and scraping on rocks was avoided at all cost. The voyageurs were absolutely forbidden to run certain rapids. Portages were the hardest part of the trip, especially in the fall, when the canoes were heavily laden with furs. Every man was expected to carry two bales, each weighing 90 pounds, and he took them over the portage at a trot.

No voyageur ever dipped a paddle in the Nulhegan River, but the Nulhegan watershed is voyageur country in spirit if not in fact. Like Maine, it belongs to the big north woods. The St. Francis Indians used the Nulhegan on their annual migration to the seacoast, and Rogers' Rangers may have come through here in 1759 (although some accounts put Rogers' route along the Passumpsic River). Like the valley of the White River, the Nulhegan was a natural route for a railroad, and a line was built from Portland, Maine, in 1853 to give Montréal access to an ice-free, deepwater harbor during the winter. A tremendous traffic in the exporting of Canadian grain soon developed. This has now disappeared, but the railroad still exists. Formerly the Grand Trunk Railway, it has been part of the Canadian National system since the 1920s.

I let the canoe drift down from Nulhegan Pond on the infant Nulhegan River and slipped under the railroad at milepost 145, almost halfway between Portland and Montréal. Dense alder thickets engaged my attention until I came out in an open marsh. A heron that had been sitting in a spruce flew off, making a low-pitched croaking noise, the vacated branch springing up and down behind him. Cold rain began to fall and the river went back into the alders, splitting into three narrow channels. Then the stream that drains McConnell Pond came in on the left and the Nulhegan grew wider — about one canoe length wide and almost as deep.

The rain-swollen current flowed smooth and fast, making paddling unnecessary, and as the canoe slipped silently around a bend I surprised a deer. A few seconds later I heard it jump into the river and swim to the other side. When I went around the next curve, the deer was standing by a thicket, looking back over its shoulder at me. Deer are not so common up here as in the more settled land to the south, but they do gather in large groups in the winter to seek shelter in the bogs and the cedar swamps. The Nulhegan basin provides choice deer yards, and once, over on Moose River (a tributary of the Passumpsic), I counted more than eighty deer in a single morning when I went into Victory Bog on skis. Northern deer are supposed to be bigger than their kin in southern Vermont, and these certainly looked splendid in their thick, bluish winter coats. Steam came shooting out their nostrils in smoking jets. It was so cold and still in the cedar swamp that the dry powder snow had piled up in 8-inch-high gobs on the branches, and it came down in a fine sparkling mist when I brushed against the trees. The deer had trampled the frozen, snow-covered creek into a hard-packed highway. You could have ridden a bicycle on it.

Now, on the Nulhegan, there was drizzle. I floated downstream for several more miles until I came to Wenlock Siding. The water level was at least a foot higher than it had been the day before and still rising, even though the rain had stopped. I began to wonder if it was high enough to run the rapids on the lower river. I had no intention of trying — some of the pitches are rumored to be Class IV — but it was worth taking a look, at least, so I drove down to the highway bridge at the old stone dam site.

There were dozens of log-driving dams on the Nulhegan in the old days; they are all gone now. I slipped the canoe into the water and poled upstream against a muscular current for about a mile and a half to the mouth of the Black Branch. There was a short set of rapids in another half-mile, its roar drowned out by the thunder of the real rapids, which began around the next curve. Here was gradient that you could see; if it had been any steeper you would have called it a waterfall. The Nulhegan came plunging and bubbling down a steep slope studded with white, fine-grained, round granite boulders. The naturally dark water gave the foam an evil golden tint. Big chunks of frothy suds bobbed in the eddies. Was it Class IV? Perhaps. The image that came to mind was that of falling down a staircase; I could almost feel the canoe banging and crunching on those beautiful white boulders. You might want to wear a wet suit in these rapids — and a helmet. Or you might want to forget the whole thing; the portage wouldn't be that hard. Blocks of ice coming down the river had cleared back the dense spruce woods 30 feet from either bank.

I got back in the canoe and shot through the lower rapids. A partridge flew across the river in a long, graceful glide, disappearing into the spruces, and as the roar of the whitewater faded I heard the evening freight on the Canadian National, blowing for some lonely grade crossings. The throbbing rumble of diesel units laboring upgrade grew louder and was followed by the rhythmic, surflike swish of a hundred boxcars coming along behind — paper and newsprint rolling out of the big woods. Back at the car, I drove downstream, the Nulhegan close by but out of sight in the forest. The road crossed the East Branch, and 2 miles later it came out into the sudden openness of the Connecticut Valley. I turned left on Vermont Route 102, heading upstream toward Colebrook. The storm had begun to clear, and shafts of sunlight streamed down through rips in the clouds, illuminating the fresh green hills. The damp fields had a good smell in the cool evening air, and I felt a strange sort of emptiness balling up in my stomach. This valley — this ancient green valley — was so pretty it was sad. The paved highway ended and I drove along on noisy gravel. At a pullout beside the river there was a perfect launching spot; that was where I would put the canoe in the next day.

❧

August 13. The osprey hovered, tail spread in a fan, legs pumping in time with the wingbeats, then wheeling around in a half-circle and dropping like a stone — 60 feet, straight down — striking the water with a bright splash, almost going under, just the wingtips showing above the spray, fighting to lift off and finally succeeding, a rainbow trout dangling from one talon. Two swallows darted out from the bank to chase the fish hawk. A kingfisher made a fussy little dive of its own as a cormorant flew by at high speed, its long neck stretched out, disappearing around a downstream bend; then the valley was quiet. The corn in the bottomland fields was 7 feet tall and tassled, the stalks absolutely still in the calm morning sunshine. Spruce-clad hills came down to meet the floodplain.

George Van Dyke had a railroad built here in 1887, on the New Hampshire side, but having no desire to be a rail tycoon, he sold the line to the Maine Central two years later. It was almost abandoned in 1977, but a local company was formed to take over its operations, and the train now runs once a week, the only customers of note being a feed store in Colebrook, New Hampshire, and a furniture factory in Beecher Falls, Vermont, which pretty much sums up the state of the economy in this northernmost part of the Connecticut Valley — a few cows and a lot of trees. There is some tourist business, too, mostly fishermen. The fishing is serious — rainbows, lake trout, and salmon — and anglers display a serious sense of style that might seem overblown in a lesser country, one without so many clear, fast streams and deep, cold lakes. Driving into Colebrook in the evening, down the wide main street with logging trucks parked in the side yards and dark, rising mountains looming above, it seemed like a town that was a long way from anywhere else, and its remoteness was highly becoming.

Now, out on the Connecticut in broad daylight, it was warm but not hot. The air was clear, with a hint of autumn in it, and I was feeling a little nostalgic, thinking about the river coming to an end. You could count the tributaries that were left on the fingers of one hand: the Mohawk River, Leach Creek, Halls Stream, Indian Stream, and Perry Stream. But there was still a ways to go. I went under a single-span covered bridge, and the next bend revealed a pair of harmless Class I rapids. The osprey soared overhead, searching out its next target. With his mate and two or three chicks back at the nest, an osprey has to catch four or five fish a day; he is well equipped for the job with a reversible outer toe (for carrying trout fore and aft, like a torpedo), sandpaper-like spicules on the bottom of his feet (for grasping slippery scales), nostril openings that can close, extraflexible wing joints (for hovering and liftoff power), and superb eyesight (six times as powerful as a man's). About one dive in three is successful. The largest fish that can be lifted out of the water weighs a pound and a half. The osprey himself, although he looks like a big bird, almost on the scale of an eagle, weighs only about 3½ pounds.

In the blue sky beyond the osprey, Monadnock Mountain rose up from the Vermont side of the river in a green mass, so close and big that it had no shape. Four fly fishermen stood in the shallow, glittering water of the rapids, lost in concentration, like stalking herons. Faced with this situation, with a heavily laden *canot du nord*, the voyageurs would probably have gotten out to wade, carrying as much cargo on their backs as necessary and pulling their canoe up the bony quickwater on a line. It took a little longer that way, but it was better than running the risk of having to stop, unload everything, and repair abrasion damage to the hull. These low-water, summer rapids could chew a bark canoe to shreds; indeed, while I was poling up the fastest part, another party swept by in the opposite direction, their dented aluminum canoes clanging and banging on the rocks, the paddlers laughing and shouting in French.

Above the rapids, the Connecticut settled into its familiar pattern of noisy riffles and quiet pools. I worked my way up to the Colebrook bridge and then a few miles farther, turning back in the late afternoon. Someone had been hard at it with a chain saw all day — laying in a supply of firewood, I suppose — and the nasal scream of the motor had pursued me like an insistent mosquito. At last it stopped, and a great hush seemed to descend upon the valley. The reflections in the smooth water had an unreal brilliance, more vivid than life. After a while I overtook a harried-looking mother merganser with a brood of eighteen ducklings that were almost as large as she. Many of them, no doubt, had been foisted off on her by less devoted parents. Adult mergansers cannot fly at this time of year because of the molt, and the young ducks have not yet learned how. When something excites them — the appearance of a canoe will do it — they race off across the water, rearing up and flapping their useless wings, kicking up rooster tails of spray with their churning feet.

❧

August 14. Above the mouth of the Mohawk River, near Colebrook, the Connecticut indulges itself in a final splurge of extravagant meandering; then Leach Creek (a stream that rises in Québec) enters on the Vermont side. The Canadian border is about 2 miles away. I got out on the river early, while the morning fog was still thick. There is supposed to be a rapid called the Horserace somewhere in here, but I couldn't pick it out from all the other small rapids. I could not, in fact, see 50 feet in front of the canoe.

The fog started to burn off about nine o'clock, just as the Sunday church bells began to chime, and the temperature seemed to rise 10 degrees in as many minutes. A bend in the river yielded a view of Canaan, Vermont — a couple of silvertopped silos, a white steeple, and two dozen houses in the distance. Canaan faces West Stewartstown on the New Hampshire side, where an old farmhouse near the riverbank now serves as the St. Regis Paper Company regional field office.

St. Regis, a multinational corporation headquartered in New York City, owns most of the land in the Connecticut Lakes region as well as large portions of the Nulhegan River and Paul Stream drainages — some 320,000 acres in all, about equally divided between New Hampshire and Vermont. There are no St. Regis paper mills in the area, however, and all of the woods work on St. Regis land — logging, road building, timber trucking, and so on — is contracted to jobbers or individuals. St. Regis manages to keep a fairly low profile, with only about thirty-five employees on the Vermont–New Hampshire Unit payroll. This I learned on a visit to West Stewartstown in 1982.

Peter Ludwig was the man I went to see. We talked for a while, then climbed into a powder blue company pickup to drive down the Vermont side of the valley to Bloomfield. There we crossed the Nulhegan at its mouth and turned off on a gravel road that went uphill into the forest along a noisy creek, forking every few miles, and finally stopped at a muddy clearing. The air smelled of sawdust and diesel fuel. There were piles of logs and men working with chain saws. Peter handed me a yellow hard hat, pulled on a pair of rubber boots, and set off into the woods on a skidder trail.

"Wilson's warbler," he said, pointing to a momentary flash of color in the underbrush. Peter is a soft-spoken, watchful man in his mid-forties, with short hair and sharp features, a native of Maine. He chewed on a birch twig as he walked, pausing now and then to look around and whack stumps with his light cruising ax. Testing the wood, I suppose. The way a stand of timber is cut determines, to a large extent, the way it grows back. Peter was visualizing these woods fifty years from now. He pointed out mistakes the loggers had made, things they had done right.

"We switched from stumpage to cut-and-haul a few years ago," Peter said. "It gives us more control and it's better for the contractors. It eliminates the feast-or-famine aspect." St. Regis deals with as many as thirty or thirty-five local contractors. A few still use horses, a good woods horse being indispensable in certain types of logging, but most contractors have invested heavily in expensive equipment. A new skidder, for example, can cost as much as $130,000. The landowner-contractor relationship is a touchy subject in the north country, since big companies like St. Regis are dealing from a position of strength while the contractors pretty much have to take whatever work they can get. The result is that the logger is probably not paid as much as he feels he deserves. On the other hand, it is not in the interest of the landowner to strike too hard a bargain lest it drive the contractors out of business. Also, a contractor who is teetering on the verge of bankruptcy will cut corners, to the ultimate detriment of the paper company's primary asset — the forest and the land itself.

Peter and I got back in the pickup and started out the road that had brought us in, taking one of the forks and heading deeper into the woods, going up and down hills and rattling over creeks on log bridges. Peter pointed out some bear tracks in the dirt, and once in a great while a long view would open up at the top of a rise, but mostly I was looking at trees — spruce and fir in the valleys, maple and yellow birch on the higher side-hills, and pure stands of paper birch, canoe birch, on some of the old burns. Virtually all of this land was cut over in the nine-teenth and early twentieth centuries; there are no significant commercial-grade virgin stands left anywhere in New England. When really large timbers are needed for a special project, such as the Saxtons River covered bridge, they come from Washing-ton or Oregon. Later in the afternoon, however, we visited an 80-acre stand of virgin spruce and fir near the Second Connect-icut Lake that the CVLC loggers had left alone, first by accident, then to preserve it as a curiosity. At first sight it was a little disappointing. I had expected giant patriarchs, and these trees, though certainly not small, were not overwhelming. Once a spruce tree up here reaches a certain size it doesn't get much bigger, it just gets older. These had been on the stump for three or four hundred years. They were growing here when Adrian Block sailed up the Connecticut in 1614. Sadly, spruce budworm is claiming some of them now.

At an active cut nearby, Peter picked up a spruce bough and whacked it with his ax, making a dozen budworm caterpillars dangle down on silk threads. Outbreaks of budworm or dis-eases such as birch dieback, not to mention unpredictable shifts in the market or slumps in the economy, can put a crimp in a forester's long-range plans, and long-range planning is impera-tive. It takes a stand of timber about fifty or sixty years to reach harvestable size up here, which means that in order to maintain a sustainable yield, St. Regis cuts only about 2 to 3 percent of its land in a given year, the size and type of the cuts depending on the condition of the trees and what they will be used for — pulpwood, veneer logs, dimension lumber, railroad ties, chips, or whatever. The most intensive kind of logging is whole-tree chipping. We stopped at a clear cut near Paul Stream where every tree had been snipped off at the ground by a set of shears called a feller-buncher and then placed in piles. A truck-mounted crane fed the trees butt-first into the shrieking jaws of the shipper, and I stood there watching as an entire birch tree disappeared into the front of the machine while chips came flying out the back in a steady stream. It took about fifteen minutes. Whole-tree chipping is best suited to low-grade stands of rough and rotten trees that would otherwise be useless. There is concern, however, that removing the limbs and branches — the slash left behind in conventional logging — may rob the soil of nutrients.

Driving from one site to the next, I soon lost all sense of direction. None of the private logging roads are marked. They don't follow drainage patterns, and they don't go anyplace in particular, aside from the various sites. Road building, Peter said, is the most expensive part of logging, and good roads are obviously essential now that river driving and logging railroads have been phased out. A brand-new road was going in on the North Branch of the Nulhegan, on International Paper Company land, with a D8L Caterpillar bulldozer doing the preliminary work. A D8L is a big machine weighing 55 tons. It grunted and churned back and forth in the dirt like a big old grizzly bear rooting out groundhogs. Boulders clanged on the blade, shivered, and rolled aside. Trees toppled like toothpicks. The freshly exposed earth, moist and black, smelled wonderful. The operator looked very small, perched up in the driver's seat with a silvery halo of horseflies swirling around his head. He was sitting on a heap of north woods logging history. Among other things, the road networks have made logging camps a thing of the past (except in the most remote parts of Maine). A lot of the romance has gone out of logging, although some of the old-time rivermen would have claimed that there was precious little romance to begin with.

Sunday the fourteenth of August was a good day to be out on the Connecticut in a canoe. A few last wisps of morning fog still hung in the blue sky above the mountains as I poled by the St. Regis office up through riffles that continued to the Canaan–West Stewartstown highway bridge, where I took out on the Vermont side. Above the bridge the riverbed was dry rock, the flow diverted into a large wooden penstock that runs along the Vermont bank for a quarter-mile from the Canaan Dam to the little Public Service Company of New Hampshire powerhouse. I drove up past the dam and through the village of Beecher Falls, where the railroad ends at the Ethan Allen furniture factory. Halls Stream, which forms the border between Québec and New Hampshire before flowing through a narrow sliver of Vermont to join the Connecticut, came in on the left. In fact, Halls Stream — or Rivière Hall, as it's called in Québec — is the *only* tributary that touches both Vermont and New Hampshire.

I continued up the Connecticut, and the hard road turned to gravel before I stopped to examine a granite monument bearing this inscription:

SUPREME COURT
OF THE
UNITED STATES
1934

The Northeast Corner of Vermont
Is A Point At The Low Water Mark
On The West Side Of The Connecticut
River in Lat. 45 00'49.20" Long.
71 27'57.48"M, 89 48'E. 312 feet
From The Center Of This Marker

The 45th parallel, of course, is halfway between the Equator and the North Pole. A bronze disk in the top of the monument identified it as border marker number 90, the last one.

A little farther up the road, still on the west bank but in New Hampshire, I parked the car in the grass and let the canoe down a steep drop to the river's edge. The valley is constricted here, with forested hills on either side. A fresh breeze ruffled the leaves, and the water was deep blue, gurgling and hissing over stones, many of which were blazed with streaks of paint or bright smears of aluminum where canoes had scraped. The voyageurs would have been mortified. I began working my way upstream, easily at first, then with more difficulty as the gradient steepened and the waves grew larger. The only feasible route appeared to be a narrow chute where the full force of the current surged between two boulders in a powerful, turbulent V. I was leery of attempting it, but there was no other choice, and in an instant the canoe was sideways. It glanced off one rock and crashed into another, sticking fast. The gunwale began to dip, and I hopped out on a third rock, allowing the canoe to slip free before it had a chance to swamp.

The problem here was one of composure; I had allowed myself to panic. Now I got back in the canoe and inched up into the V, the bow splitting the current like a knife blade. That was the critical thing: the angle of the bow. As long as I kept the angle I could hold the canoe here all day. It didn't take a lot of force, just constant attention. But this is a hard lesson to learn. With the river roaring in your ear, with the water pounding and foaming on big rocks, every instinct in your body screams at you to hang on for dear life, to move fast, *to get out of here in a hurry*, which is exactly what you cannot do. Now, more than ever, you want a light touch, a measured, methodical plan of attack. You have to deal with the rapid the way a craftsman shapes a piece of wood, whittling it down to size slowly but surely. I lifted the pole off the riverbed and planted it again, taking the time to fit the butt securely into a socket-like niche between two bottom stones, and *then* I shoved hard, but with a smooth, even pressure, hand over hand up the pole three times, the final thrust driving the canoe up the steepest part of the V with momentum to spare.

The rapids went on and on, but there were perfect resting places in the numerous eddies; the canoe seemed almost to seek them out on its own accord, nosing up to the sheltering rocks like a friendly dog as I ferried back and forth across the river, feeling out a course through the maze. After 3 miles of this I came to smooth water. Indian Stream, which rises way up on the Québec border, farther north than the Connecticut River itself, came in on the left. The Indian Stream watershed is hilly and forested, accessible only by private logging roads and virtually uninhabited except for a cluster of dairy farms at the mouth. Even though this is cold country for agriculture, or for anything else, both Great Britain and the United States claimed it after the Revolution. Nothing was done to settle the dispute until a group of settlers took matters into their own hands and established the Indian Stream Republic, printing money and raising a militia. The republic lasted for three years, becoming part of New Hampshire in 1835.

Above the mouth of Indian Stream the rapids on the Connecticut resumed, gradually increasing in difficulty until a staircase series of creamy white falls barred the way. I walked the last little bit along the bank and climbed up on an old wooden bridge to watch a pair of fly fishermen work the boiling pool at the foot of the cascade. The sun made little rainbows in the mist and the spray. The village of Pittsburg and a large, manmade reservoir called Lake Francis are about a mile upstream, and beyond that are the four Connecticut Lakes. The first two, good-size bodies of water to begin with, were made larger by the NEPCO dams at their outlets. The Third Lake is not nearly so big, and the Fourth Lake is a tiny pond. It is the source of the Connecticut River.

The elevation of the Fourth Lake is 2,600 feet. Lake Francis is 1,380 feet. Thus the river drops 1,220 feet in a straight distance of less than 20 miles. This, in other words, is the steep part of the long profile. Above the Second Lake the Connecticut is too small to float a canoe, and between Second Lake and First Lake as well as between First Lake and Lake Francis the gradient is severe, with several pitches that must be portaged. High water is a necessity, but too much water makes it dangerous. For all practical purposes, the falls below Pittsburg are the head of canoe navigation — except, of course, on the lakes themselves. I had come to the end of the line.

15 🖎 HEADWATERS

I WOKE UP, as planned, at five A.M. Dim gray light showed outside the tent. The Connecticut River, just a little brook way up here between the Third and the Second Connecticut Lakes, gurgled down its rocky bed.

I got in the car and drove out to the highway. Sue Weingarten was with me. We turned off on a St. Regis gravel road that crossed the river and then ran alongside it, the water glimmering faintly through the trees, growing wide and placid as it approached the inlet to the Second Lake. I parked on the shoulder, pulled on hip boots, and carried the canoe down a path that ended in black, sucking mud. Susie took the bow and we shoved off.

Lush stands of marsh grass grew along both sides of the inlet, and a very slight mist rose off the water. Off in the distance an empty logging truck came down the highway from Canada, winding through ten gears; the noise faded away. A family of mergansers swam ahead of the canoe, skittering off to the side as we went around a bend where the inlet opened up into a bay and a young bull moose stood in the shallows. The moose looked up, hesitated, and broke into a trot, splashing at first, then swimming as it hit deeper water, finally climbing out on the far shore of the bay and looking back before disappearing into thick spruce woods, breaking branches as it went.

We paddled out to the lake and examined a beaver lodge on the shore. The dawn was coming up gray and murky. I tried to tell myself that one moose, glimpsed from a distance, was satisfactory, but of course it wasn't. This was supposed to be moose city up here. Maybe I had chosen the wrong spot. Or the wrong morning. We swung the canoe around and started back.

Just then a great black bull emerged from the woods, striding purposefully out into the middle of the bay. He looked at us intently and then began to feed on bottom weeds. I paddled a few strokes toward the moose and paused for a reaction. There was none. I let the canoe drift. The moose had his head underwater, and when he came up for air he snorted, spraying mist. Susie twisted around in her seat.

"Please don't go any closer," she whispered. We could hear the moose chewing. Thin green strands of grass hung out of his mouth. He was standing belly-deep in water, and when he put his head under, only the tines of his antlers showed above the surface. Then he would raise that huge, heavy head and the water would drain off it in glassy sheets, pouring back into the lake. From time to time he took a few steps, hunching down to submerge his back, then standing up straight and shaking himself to get rid of flies. After a while a second moose came down to the shore. This new moose checked out the canoe, glanced at the big bull, and began to feed at a respectful distance. Moose are basically solitary animals, but they are not territorial; they can stand each other's company, within limits. In the fall, of course, the bulls fight.

❧

From where Susie and I sat in the canoe, looking at the moose, the state of Maine was 5¼ miles due west. The headwaters of the Little Magalloway River are just across the line. Spruce and fir forest extends in a northwesterly direction for 90 miles to Moosehead Lake and Greenville, Maine, and then north for another 100 miles to the St. John River. It is standard north woods country — cold, damp, and lonely — but it is not wilderness. There is no wilderness left in New England. There is not much big wilderness left in the United States, and there are no wild rivers. A few rivers do have wild sections or wild tributaries, but to find rivers that are wild from headwaters to ocean it is necessary to go to Alaska or Canada. Northern Québec is the wilderness canoeist's promised land. A quick look at the map is enough to bring on a fever. Even in Canada, however, technology has changed the rules. Ever since the float plane replaced the canoe as the primary means of long-distance travel in the north woods, the wilderness has lost much of its forbidding size, much of its danger. But just because you can fly in to some remote lake, does that mean it is not wilderness? What if there is a trapper's cabin on the lake? What if there is an oil rig? Wilderness can be hard to define. Clearly, however, it has to have a certain quality and a certain minimum size. A hundred acres is not enough. What about ten thousand acres? Does the land have to be pristine or can it have been logged over at some point in the past? Roads are not permissible in wilderness, but what about a pipeline? Or a graded hiking trail? What about some particularly popular area, such as the Middle Fork of the Salmon River, where private parties have to make reservations a year in advance, drawing their permits in a lottery? Could that possibly be wilderness? There is not much agreement about any of this, and the debate, while not pointless, can get tiresome. I know, in my own mind, what wilderness is, and any lingering doubts were banished in 1976 when Chris Ayres and I went down the Noatak River in northern Alaska.

In the Inupiat Eskimo language Noatak means "deep inside." The Noatak River rises of glacial melt deep inside the Brooks Range and flows in a westerly direction to the Chukchi Sea, an arm of the Arctic Ocean near the Bering Strait. There is one small Eskimo village (population, 250) on the lower Noatak, but aside from that, nothing. There are no bridges, dams, roads, airstrips, or satellite tracking stations. The country is essentially unchanged since the day the ancestors of the Paleo-Indians crossed over from Siberia and pitched their caribou-skin tents on the tundra.

The length of the Noatak River and the size of its drainage basin are roughly equal to those of the Connecticut, and while these similarities are striking, so are the differences. The Noatak is entirely above the Arctic Circle. It flows through stark, barren land and stunted, scrubby spruce forest at the extreme northern limit of tree growth. On the other hand, New England during the waning stages of the most recent glaciation was at least as cold and bleak as Alaska is today, and the Noatak country, with its tundra and caribou, its Eskimo inhabitants and retreating glaciers in the headwater mountains, is a fairly authentic model of the postglacial, Paleo-Indian Connecticut Valley. The great meltwater lakes are missing, as are the mastodons and mammoths, but the primitive quality is intact.

Russian fur traders and Yankee whalers visited the mouth of the Noatak fairly early, but white men did not even get a look at the interior of the Noatak basin until just before World War I, when an army mapping expedition worked its way upstream in small boats. Chris Ayres and I arrived at the Noatak headwaters in a chartered float plane less than forty-eight hours after leaving New York City in a jumbo jet. My primary reaction was one of relief. We had made it; the hard part of the trip was behind us. We sat down and poured a drink, then caught some fish. Cottongrass blew in the wind. There were big, nameless mountains all around, with nameless creeks tumbling down the side valleys. Wilderness is supposed to be soothing. This was. Three days passed before we could even think about getting in the canoe. I spent the time in a trance, marveling at the size and the emptiness of the country.

But once the actual journey down the river got under way

(it was to take us nearly a month), the focus of my personal world narrowed. With nothing more pressing to worry about than wet socks, wet socks became important. With unlimited daylight at our disposal, we kept to a voyageur-style schedule, sometimes paddling fourteen hours at a stretch. We wolfed down the evening meal, slept like the dead, and got up the next day to do it all over again. Food became an obsession. Our major regret was that we had no shotgun for the ducks, although Chris did get a ptarmigan with his .30-30 carbine, shooting the bird neatly through the eye (and removing its head). Fortunately, the Noatak teemed with fish — grayling in the upper reaches, salmon and Arctic char downstream.

Some things were not as I expected. Mosquitoes were never much of a nuisance. Wildlife, aside from the incredibly abundant waterfowl, was scarce. One afternoon we saw a wolverine turning over rocks, and during the course of an overnight hike up into the hills we found a fine herd of Dhall sheep. Still, that didn't seem like much. Not for Alaska. I had expected living rivers of caribou. We saw only three, three caribou in a month. One of them was an abandoned yearling that came trotting up to greet us, then fled to the far end of the island where it was apparently stranded, afraid to swim the river by itself. There it would stay until it starved to death or a wolf took it. For me that summed up the Noatak barrenlands. It was a protean, wind-beaten landscape, sprinkled with bleached bones and bright with tiny flowers. The morning after we saw the yearling we found fresh grizzly tracks in front of the tent.

Late one stormy afternoon, a little less than halfway into the trip, we came to the mouth of the Cutler River and climbed to the top of some high bluffs for the view. The Cutler is the Noatak's major tributary. It is a fifth-order stream, about the size of the White River. There are some tall bluffs behind the American Legion hall in White River Junction, and I have often stood up there, looking down at the confluence of the White and the

Connecticut. But this was not Vermont. There was no B&M Railroad, no Coolidge Hotel, no I-91. There was nothing manmade here except our silver canoe, down on a gravel bar. The Noatak's broad waters were green and clouded. The Cutler ran clear as a limestone spring. There were vacant views for at least 75 miles in every direction, out to the dead mountains in the distance. The tundra's dull brown hide seemed perfectly mated to the somber dome of cold sky. We sat and stared. There were no words for this country, no clues. You could run your mind over it a thousand different ways and come up empty every time. The soul rejects terminal nothingness. The thought of permanent exile in such a bleak, ultimately lonely place goes against all instinct.

And yet the emptiness is precious, too, an affirmation of something important, perhaps even of life itself. All life comes from nothingness; the empty Noatak horizon seemed full of promise. At the very least, Chris and I knew that we still had more than 200 miles of wild river left to travel, and it was a thought to be savored. I have remembered the moment many times since, always with pleasure.

Often, while out on the Connecticut River, I have tried to conjure up a vision of the wild, primeval valley that was once there, and the memory of the Noatak was helpful in that. It was helpful, too, in seeing the wildness that exists in the Connecticut even yet, for there is much of it. There is wildness in the flight of the swallow, in the slap of a beaver's tail. There is wildness in the cold winter sky, in the rumble of the rapids, and in the blind determination of the alewives struggling upstream against the current. There is wildness in the ancient, waterworn stone and in the mountains heaved up by moving continents. There is wildness in the Connecticut River, in all rivers. Wildness is the engine that drives all nature. It is as powerful as the force that grinds potholes in solid rock, as delicate as the tread of the water strider. It is subtle, complex, all-encompassing, without soul or morality, locked into immutable laws, like the flow of the river itself. Man has interfered with it, bending it to his uses, and the extent of his industry is remarkable, given the short time in which it has been accomplished; still, nothing fundamental has changed. We have built the dams, but the flow is not stopped; the hydrologic cycle continues as before. We have done a little remodeling, a little tinkering, created some small moments of beauty, and made a little mess. It is only arrogance that makes it seem like something more. Inevitably, the wildness in this river has been diluted, but it will never be extinguished.

❧

One more moose story. It was the middle of August. I was driving down to the Second Connecticut Lake in the evening when I saw a van with Québec plates parked by the logging road bridge across the inlet creek (the infant Connecticut River). There was a canoe on the roof of the van, so I stopped to ask the driver if he was taking out or putting in. I was planning to look for moose, and if there was going to be another canoe on the water, I thought I might try a different spot.

"Be my guest," the man said. "We're leaving." Then he added, "But the moose, she don't spook easy."

I slipped my canoe into the inlet and drifted on down to the lake in the deepening twilight. Sure enough, there was a cow moose standing in the water, feeding on bottom weeds. I tried to be very quiet at first, but it was a wasted effort. This moose couldn't have cared less about me. She scarcely seemed to be aware of my presence. I watched her for about half an hour, until it began to get dark; then the French canoe approached from upstream. Apparently they had changed their minds. There were three of them, two men and a boy. I sat there, astonished, as they nosed their craft up to the moose. I thought I had been close; this crew came to within 3 or 4 feet. I could see the headline: ENRAGED MOOSE TRAMPLES CANOEISTS. Then the man in the bow stood up, took a small camera out of his pocket, and proceeded to take a picture. When the flashbulb popped in the moose's face, her eyes shone like big orange marbles. She blinked once and stuck her head back underwater for another mouthful of weeds. Business as usual.

The cow was still there, in the same spot, at five-thirty the next morning. The sun was just beginning to probe through the tops of the spruce trees, and it made the wispy plumes of fog rising off the inlet look like golden smoke. Loons were wailing out on the lake. The moose was a dark shadow in the glowing mist, ethereal yet undeniably solid and huge, its ears alert, and diamond droplets of water glittering on the brown hide. I settled into serious picture taking, cranking off sixty or seventy frames, using both cameras and every lens I owned, from the 28mm wide angle to the 500mm mirror telephoto. If I had had more film, I would have taken more pictures. I couldn't stop myself. Then a second moose came out of the woods. A few minutes later a third moose appeared. Each time I looked into the viewfinder I grew more excited. Moose have been described as homely, slow-witted, awkward, a mismatched assemblage of spare parts. Not true. A moose, in the proper north woods setting, is majestic. He *is* the north woods, no less than the raven or the wolf. Far from clumsy, a moose can move with power and grace over terrain that would leave a strong man floundering. A big bull in motion is fluid and unstoppable, balancing his great rack of antlers as deftly as a waiter with a tray of brimming champagne glasses.

I had worked myself into such a fever over the possibilities of moose photography that I returned to the Connecticut Lakes region on August 24. Unfortunately, the Second Lake had been drawn down for the winter in my absence, and the main inlet was now a little creek running through dry mudflats. I decided to switch my attention to a long, narrow pond about a mile up the East Inlet stream. With a small New Hampshire Fish & Game Department dam of its own, it was not affected by the water level in the lake.

I launched the canoe shortly after five o'clock on the morning of the twenty-fifth. It had been a cold, clear night and the grass was sopping with dew when I got up. Now the pond was making heavy fog — another disappointment — and as the sun rose the fog grew thicker. I couldn't see a thing; there was no point in even taking the cameras out of the pack basket. I let the canoe glide to a stop on the glassy water, and a raven croaked somewhere in the distance. Ducks flew overhead, mergansers by the sound of their wings. Was the molt finished yet? Then I heard a moose splashing, walking through the shallows, *very* close but invisible. He must have caught my scent because the splashing stopped. I could almost picture the animal, his head raised, testing the air. Then the moose snorted. The splashing began again, urgently, followed by the noise of breaking branches — and silence.

If there was one moose on the pond, there might be others; I would wait. Suddenly the bull — it was a huge bull with a full rack — burst out of the woods, hit the water with a crash, and swam in front of me at full speed, churning up a tremendous wake that left the canoe rocking. I saw him for only a second or two before he vanished back into the fog. It was like a freight train passing. The waves were still lapping on the shore.

The fog started to burn off a little later, and I went down to the far end of the pond, into the marshy part, putting up ducks and surprising a cow moose with two calves. The three of them fled while I was still several hundred yards off. Nothing was going right. I tried taking pictures of birds, but I couldn't get close enough. Then, just as I was about to bite into a maple-frosted doughnut, an otter surfaced beside the canoe. He dove as I reached for the camera. This was awful; I headed back toward the car. As I was poling along the shore a deer stepped into a small clearing and stood still long enough for the first picture of the day, a meager consolation prize. The deer twitched his big pie plate ears and bolted, snorting as he went — that high-pitched, barking kind of snort that deer sometimes make — and I had to laugh. What was I feeling so aggrieved about? In the span of two hours I had seen four moose, a deer, an otter, and three kinds of duck, a cormorant, herons, king-fishers, ravens, and a little pied-billed grebe. The Noatak couldn't compare.

As the sun grew warmer, an old silvery snag that stuck out of the water began to attract cedar waxwings. They would land on it, sit for a few seconds, then fly off. The cedar waxwing is an enchanting bird, with a fawn-colored body, a pert crest, and a dark mask across the eyes. The tail ends with a bright yellow stripe, as if it had been dipped in a can of paint. The waxwings paid no attention to me, and when the cry of a hawk floated down out of the sky they ignored that, too. I glassed the clouds with the big lens and spotted a red-tailed hawk circling above a clear cut in the distance. Swinging the camera down to the level of the water, I found a little round snipe busy in the marsh grass by the shore, jabbing the mud with its long, slender bill. According to some people, clear cuts have boosted the moose population while thinning out the deer, the theory being that moose like the open browse and can handle the deep snow (which would bog a deer down). And it wouldn't be too long before the snow started to fly. Although the raspberries were still ripe, the maples on the hillside had already begun to turn. Summer was over.

❧

Above the Second Lake, the Connecticut River is shallow enough so that you can wade right up the middle of it, and at one point the entire flow is held back by a beaver dam. The public road from Pittsburg to the Canadian border was not built until 1937, as a make-work Civilian Conservation Corps project, and it was not paved until 1960. The day I drove up to the customs post, in October, only three cars had crossed ahead of me, about average for that time of year.

The Third Lake nestles against the border at an elevation of 2,191 feet. The U.S. and the Canadian customs stations are up on a saddle in the ridge above the north end of the lake. Both are one-man operations, closed at night. When I went into the American building, the fellow in charge was stirring a pan of chicken soup. I asked him for directions to the Fourth Lake.

"Just walk up the hill there," he said, pointing out the back window. "Follow the border for a mile and you can't miss it. There's a red arrow on a tree."

I began climbing. The border is a 40-foot-wide corridor cut out of the forest along the crest of the ridge. Snow from an early storm lingered on the ground in shady places, and the mountain ashes had clusters of bright red berries. Every few minutes, it seemed, a partridge would explode out of the underbrush, always surprising me. To the north, the land fell away sharply for 600 or 700 feet and leveled off into gently rolling hills, with the tiny village of Chartierville, Québec, in the distance. To the south, as I had been told, a red arrow pointed the way to Fourth Lake. There was the faint suggestion of a trail at first, but it petered out in old-growth spruce woods where the ground was soft and springy underfoot, the walking easy and quiet. Then the Fourth Lake appeared, down in a slight hollow.

"All the rivers run into the sea," it says in Ecclesiastes, "yet the sea is not full; unto the place from whence the rivers come, thither they return again." This was the place. The Fourth Lake was about an acre and a half in extent, fringed with brown marsh grass. Fragile plates of ice floated in the shallows. The water was blue, slightly ruffled in the wind. Some ravens soared above the ridge, calling back and forth, and after a while they went away. A very old beaver dam, overgrown with grass and bushes, stretched across the lake's outlet. I walked out on the dam and stood there, listening to the sound of running water.